PRAISE

"In *When Blood Matters*, Dana weaves a beautiful tapestry of DNA and God's destiny, relating her story to the cry in every person's heart: Who am I, really? Her transparency with her own struggles and victories is so refreshing. Every person will relate to her journey, no matter where they are in life. You will leave this story feeling like you've experienced the journey of real life with your best friend."

—Marla Swandt

"This is the nearly unbelievable story of a young woman who, while appearing to have it all, can't shake the feeling of being less-than and unwanted. This God-orchestrated symphony of searching, healing, and forgiving will bring hope and restoration to your soul."

—Dianne Staats

"*When Blood Matters* is a true must-read, a story of one woman's intriguing journey of healing and discovery that motivates and captivates! Dana Sellars has an undeniable gift for sharing her heart struggles and courageous journey in ways that strengthen and equip the lives of others. This book is endearing, provides hope, and will bless you each time you read it!"

—Maria Horchner

"This is a book of stories about real life. It is a book about hope and about a big God who heals and brings light into the dark spaces. It is a read-in-one-sitting, ignore-all-your-responsibilities kind of book, and I hope you will do just that. Only once you do, be prepared to come away changed."

—Staci King

"Dana Sellars delivers a stirring yet delightful insight illustrating her walk with Christ throughout her life. She experienced unimaginable tragedy, paralyzing fear of rejection, and lifelong insecurities. They served as the architecture that shaped the Godly woman she no doubt is today. Somehow, complex and chaotic situations are presented with the clarity of ringing bells. Sometimes barely tinkling; other times with a thunderous toll."

—**Charlie Hill**

"Dana writes in such an open, honest, and revealing way! She brings any and all junk into the light and then sheds God's light gloriously across it! This book is not just a story about her story and how God walked her through every step of it, but it is a story of healing, freedom, and forgiveness to which we all can relate! She reminds us that freedom through God is a real thing and He offers it to all who seek Him!"

—**Jenn Boyd**

"In *When Blood Matters*, Dana invites you into one of the most difficult discoveries of her life and shares her journey from overcoming the feelings of rejection and lack to acceptance and wholeness as a daughter of the King. As one who had the privilege and honor of walking with her through this journey, I too was able to work through my own feelings of being less-than and into the revelation of perfect love from our Heavenly Father. That's what Dana does. She invites you to "do life" with her, to experience and share the deepest, darkest parts all the way to the most freeing, celebratory ones. I am blessed to call her a friend and a sister of the heart."

—**Marci Harper**

"God's grace is undeniable. Knowing the author as a mature woman of God and hearing this story results in no other explanation but His grace for the joyful and successful life she lives."

—**Gary Staats**

"*When Blood Matters* is a story about Dana's journey to her personal "victory party"! The stories she shares with openness, honesty, and vulnerability will lead you to examine those places in your own life that sometimes seem to strangle you. None of the stories were new to me. I have witnessed them unfold in her life and have seen the pain and struggle that they introduced. What is new is the peace and freedom with which they are shared and the victory that is now hers to claim! You are invited. Come to her party and see if you need to begin planning your own "victory party"!"

—**Vickie Otts**

"Dana's story is inspirationally moving, emotionally riveting, and faith-provoking. My heart was captured by her story and the raw transparency she exhibited when I interviewed her to include it as one of the chapters in my book, *Origins*. God Himself led Dana to connect the dots generationally and genetically to her early childhood roots of rejection. That journey resulted in family reconciliation and her own personal freedom from rejection. Dana's story is no less than miraculous. I assure you that her book will inspire new faith in God's ability to transform your life as you pursue your own pathway of healing."

—**Linda Godsey** Freedom Minister, speaker, consultant, author of *Letting Go* and *Origins*

"This is a God-story like none I have read before. This true story is intriguing and delightful! Come along as Dana shares the intimate details of her journey to truth, love, and total acceptance."

—**Chrystal Sturm**

"Family is such an amazing concept. God set in motion a series of relationships that were meant to create places of safety and love. Yet our humanity often interferes. Who hasn't known the pain of feeling like you don't belong or experienced the rejection of being unwanted? In When Blood Matters, Dana Sellars exposes the symptoms and the consequences of experiencing such pain. As she shares her own journey of family healing, she teaches us that the acceptance of God's blood is so deep, wide, and significant that it can heal our human pain, suffering, and loss. If you've ever felt that you were discarded or unacceptable, you will be transformed by this story and by the revelation of God's love for you. Come along on the journey from chaos to order, loss to gain, and rejection to belonging."

—**Jan Greenwood** Pastor, Gateway Church Equip; author of Women at War

WHEN BLOOD MATTERS

When Blood Matters

HOW I UNEARTHED THE ROOT OF MY REJECTION AND DISCOVERED WHAT FAMILY REALLY MEANS

DANA SELLARS

For my parents.
I am thankful to be your daughter.

TABLE OF CONTENTS

FOREWORD

by Brooke Sailer

Have you ever gotten lost? I get lost all the time. I can be going on a short nature walk and suddenly find myself deep into the woods, very unsure of how to get out. Oh, and it's not that I can't ask for directions. That's not it at all. It's that even with a map, a compass, or, let's be real, an iPhone, I think I'm following directions until it yells, "Re-routing. Re-routing. Please proceed to the route," and oops! I realize I've done it again. I've gotten off course, even with the best of intentions.

Life is like this. There's not a road map. Or at least, not a perfect one. Even those with good motivations look up, only see the bright sun in the sky, and are unable to make out a path in the woods. Lost. Deeply so.

How did I get here? And where do I go now?

I don't know how to mentally and emotionally prepare you to hear Dana's story. I just don't. It's big. It's so big. This story you're about to read is shocking, unusual, maybe even awkward at times, deeply sad, painful, and perhaps even grievous. Yet simultaneously, I'd be lying if I didn't admit I find it oddly hopeful.

This real story is the life of an adult woman who found herself at a fork in the road as a mystery revealed itself unexpectedly, offering a way home.

Dana pours her heart into sharing the gut-wrenching details of her parents upbringing, marriages, and abuses, as well as the bits of her own childhood curiosities that overlap with the heartbreak of those who raised her. As you read, you will witness her attempts to present you with the entire story: the beginning, middle, and end. And as it unfolds page by page, she weaves in lessons, help, and hope for those feeling displaced and rejected.

My greatest hope for you is that you see how she navigated this unique journey so gracefully and that her example and perspective move you to face any surprise, trauma, unearthing, or uprooting in your own life with similar determination. If Dana can walk this road and come out stronger, more forgiving, and more whole, then so can we.

You're not going to close the final page and forget such a real story. You're going to be glad you took the time to remember that every family tree can be a forest of lost souls, *but not all is lost.* You don't even have to go searching for the directions, answers, or a way out, because the One who knows will happily find you.

INTRODUCTION

MAKING LEMONADE

Most of us are familiar with the saying, "When life gives you lemons, make lemonade." Throughout my forty-plus years of life, circumstances and events have presented many lemons, sometimes even an orchard full. I didn't necessarily need these lemons, and I certainly wasn't asking for them, but there they appeared in a disheveled box on my doorstep and confronted me with a life-altering decision to make: I could let them rot, becoming discolored with mold and disintegrating with stench; or I could put them to use.

Instead of allowing the lemons to sour my life and my taste buds, I grabbed a lot of water (tears), added tons of sugar (grace, love, and forgiveness), and prepared the biggest batch of lemonade that is still refreshing me today. This is my journey. It's a messy one. It's a journey saturated with deep pain, earth-shaking excitement, and most touchingly, God's unending mercy and redemption. This is my story of freedom. This is my story of forgiveness. This is my story of family—and what it means to be family. Most of all, it's my story of hope! God proved faithful in both my darkest moments and my most thrilling discoveries.

This book is not meant to entertain you, although I believe some will be entertained. This book is not meant to make you feel sad, although I believe some will cry. This book is a God-ordained story that reveals His majesty. In every moment, no matter how we *feel*, one truth remains.

God is good, all the time!

Although I remain blown away by my story each time I share it, my prayer is that this isn't just a cool story you ingest, only to forget in a few weeks. My desire is that you encounter and embrace the same hope that infiltrates my experience detailed in these pages. I want you to feel encouraged in your own individual, unique journey. I want you to search for your own calling within the story God is writing in your life.

What are your lemons?

I am not claiming to have recalled every detail with infallible accuracy. However, I took great care to ensure the information is honest. These are my authentic memories about my life. These are my sincere interpretations of and feelings about specific scenes that have played across the big screen of my childhood and adult life. Out of respect for some people in my life, both old and new characters, I have purposely omitted or changed some names. That being said, I have done my best to represent the entirety of this story with grace, love, and truth. The way we perceive our lives and the experiences within them remain our truth, but not necessarily someone else's truth. Some people you'll become acquainted with in this story may not agree with everything recorded. Some might say it happened differently. They might tell you a version of this very same story through their completely unique lens. But these are my memories, my emotions, my thoughts, and my revelations.

Chapter One

HUMBLE BEGINNINGS

Each of us enters the world by two people who carry their own experiences with them along their journey. Whether we were raised by two parents or one, their entire lives (including the years they lived before our existence) have a direct impact on our own life. In order for you to more fully understand my journey, it is first necessary to understand my parents' journeys, both separate and together.

My parents, Freddie and Lana, married at a very young age, even by the standards of the time. When they started their family, my dad had just turned sixteen and my mom was nineteen. I think they married for love, but marriage also offered each of them an escape from their unpleasant childhoods. Both of my parents walked a tragic road to adulthood. Neither one of them was raised in a stable home. And that's putting it politely.

MY MOM

My mom grew up under the reign of an extremely violent father whose love for alcohol overshadowed his love for his family. Estes beat his wife, Doris, every weekend for seventeen years of her life, and well into their children's lives. There was rarely peace in their home. During the week, Estes didn't drink, so Doris received a reprieve from the atrocious physical abuse. On those days, however, his obsession with control manifested in other ways.

Some days, my mom would be allowed to go outside and play; but on other days, she had to stay in the room she shared with her two siblings. Her father didn't tolerate any "silliness," you know, the basic behavior of kids being kids. He didn't like noise, so my mom and her two younger siblings would strain to be as quiet as possible, sometimes stuffing their laughing faces into pillows so he wouldn't hear them having fun. Estes had zero positive presence in their lives. He went to work, came home, ate supper, and relaxed by himself for the remainder of the evening. Then the weekends arrived along with the drinking. The more he drank, the more my grandmother would be punched, kicked, choked, slapped, and shoved. My mom, just a child, listened as her father called her mother a slew of demeaning names, some of which my mom didn't even understand at the time.

My mom lived in a constant state of fear. No one and no place was truly safe. When Doris announced she was leaving her father, my twelve-year-old mother could finally see a ray of hope rising in their lives. The only drawback of their departure was living in the same city as Estes. It wasn't far enough. He could still find them. And that's exactly what he did. One afternoon, he appeared unannounced on their front doorstep. Perhaps even more surprising was that he showed up sober. He came in the house and talked with everyone like any decent father would. Maybe he had changed? Maybe losing his family was enough to motivate his sobriety?

With this hope (and probably a dose of pity), Doris invited him over for Christmas to watch the children open their gifts. Unfortunately, his attendance shattered any hope for change or reconciliation that his previous visit prompted. That Christmas, he was not sober. And it didn't take long before something set him off and he began attacking his wife. In horror, my mom watched her mother be beaten nearly to death. My grandfather cracked my grandmother's ribs, split her lip, and left her bloody and unconscious. My mom intervened and rolled her mother's motionless body far underneath a full-size bed, out of the reach of her drunk father. They didn't own a telephone, so my mom sprinted down the snowy road and begged a neighbor to call the police. That Christmas evening, Doris spent the night in the hospital, and Estes spent the night in jail. The one Christmas miracle? It would be the very last time my mom's dad beat her mom.

I wish this was the turning point in my mom's life.

I wish her childhood was immediately rescued and renewed. Unfortunately, it only grew worse, just in a different way. Her mother found her newly single life to be fun and exciting. After all she suffered, Doris thought she deserved to have as much fun, and in whatever form, as she wished. She began staying out late, drinking heavily, and hanging around random men. My mom, then, would be left alone to care for her younger siblings. Sometimes they stayed with family, but other times they stayed with people they didn't even know, often someone her mother just met! My mom's worst memories involve her mother tucking them in at a motel room in the Fort Worth Stockyards, an area known for its multiple clubs and high crime rate. Doris locked the door to the motel room and left them there for the night. My mom begged her mother to stay with them. They felt so afraid and abandoned.

Doris jeered in reply, "Don't be so selfish, Lana! Don't you want me to be happy?"

One of the "better" places my grandmother left them for an evening was the Isis Theatre in Fort Worth. This place, meant for paid entertainment, quickly became "free childcare" for her three children. She only had to pay for entrance into the show and for popcorn and a coke for each child, which was often their only meal of the day. Sometimes an usher pitied them and sneaked them more food. My mom and her younger siblings watched the same show over and over all day until closing time. After they were dismissed from the theater, they were welcomed into a terrifying time of waiting. They never knew when, or if, their mother would come to pick them up. There were nights my mom let her siblings rest across her lap and sleep as they waited on the curb in front of the theater. A few times, their mother never showed up. On those lonely nights, they either walked miles to stay at an aunt's house or begged a taxi driver to take them home, without a penny to pay him. Luckily, only truly nice taxi drivers obliged.

My mom's life spiraled like this for years. It seems her moment of freedom was brief, as she merely left one abusive home to enter a totally negligent one. Interestingly, my mom claims the latter home life was more difficult to endure. But during my mom's sixteenth year, her mother finally settled down and married a man everyone liked. Doris and her new husband still partied, but not as much. My mom remembers these days as mostly happy times. It would be the only time in her life she felt she had a "normal" family. She managed to bury all the pain of her childhood and actually enjoyed her teen years. She was relieved that the abuse and neglect had ended, and this new marriage seemed to make her mother truly happy, for the very first time.

When Doris remarried, the family moved to a neighborhood much farther away. This seemingly insignificant move would forever impact my mom's world. As she stood in the front yard of their new house, gazing down the street, she stole her first glimpse of the man she would one day marry. Looking like a younger version of Elvis, he immediately caught my mom's attention. She was immediately smitten with his dark brown eyes, long brown hair, and summertime tan. To this day, she remembers in great detail the cut off jean shorts and the light purple Playboy Bunny t-shirt he was wearing that day. She had no idea, but he was only thirteen years old.

MY DAD

My dad's earliest memories of his childhood are fond. He always felt like a member of a pretty typical family. He had a father, Dan, and a mother, Peggy. My dad was the middle child with an older brother and a younger sister. He acknowledged that his parents tried hard to be good parents and to love one another. As a young child, he had the good fortune of rarely seeing or hearing his parents fight. His family even attended church on occasion. In a few fleeting but influential times, Dan even read the Bible to the children. My dad, being kissed goodnight by both parents nightly and without fail, felt safe and loved.

Additionally, my dad was a very gifted baseball player, which made Dan (whose favorite sport happened to be baseball) very proud. This joint love of the game provided the perfect opportunity for my dad's father to be very involved in his life. He even coached my dad's team. Peggy was greatly involved in his baseball life as well. She was known to organize fund raisers or cook corn dogs and onion rings to sell at the games. From appearances, they seemed to be an average family living in the 1950s.

But around the age of ten, my dad began to realize that they were not the Beaver, June, and Ward he thought they were. There wasn't an isolated moment of turmoil; the change was gradual. During this year, a female neighbor seemed to appear out of the blue. This particular lady started spending an unusual amount of time with my dad's family. Even after he and his siblings went to bed, their neighbor would stay over much later. My dad would peek out the window and into the backyard on these nights to find his father and this lady lying together on a pallet in the backyard. Sometimes his mother would be with them, too. They laughed loudly and obnoxiously, and my dad was annoyed by their carelessness while the kids were trying to sleep. Later on, my dad just assumed an affair was taking place. He wasn't sure if his mother didn't play a role. One afternoon, he discovered his parents' inappropriate photos in the house. Some photos were of his parents, which assumed the neighbor was behind the camera. Some were of Dan and the other woman, which assumed Peggy was behind the camera. Nevertheless, this confusing mess of a family situation marked the steady decline of the normal, stable family life my dad previously enjoyed, although his parents remained together.

Life progressed from that point without any notable occurrences until my dad was thirteen years old. One afternoon, he noticed a new family moving in just down the street from his family's home. He was thrilled when he saw a young boy in the family—a playmate! And then, he saw her. The most beautiful girl he'd ever seen. My dad undoubtedly made a point to meet that family.

He quickly struck up a friendship with my mom's younger brother. He really enjoyed spending time over at their house, especially if my mom was home. In turn, my mom tried to make sure she was home whenever her brother's "new friend" would come over. Sometimes, my bold mom would instigate the invitation herself. They quickly acknowledged the mutual interest and spent the next year seeing each other as much as possible.

But as young relationships often do, things came to an abrupt halt that summer when my dad was just fourteen years old. My dad spent that summer working at their family owned carnival. At the summer's end, his aunt, unaware of Dan and Peggy's marital issues, drove my dad home. As my dad approached his house, he noticed a random note hanging haphazardly on the front door. It read: "Go home with your aunt."

In stunned silence, he peered through the windows of his home. It was completely empty. His whole home, his whole family, his whole life purged and moved without any forewarning. Rejection engulfed my dad like a tsunami. In total confusion and shock, my dad called out to his aunt, unable to hide his desperation, "Wait, this note says I need to come to your house!"

He left for the summer with his parents together, and arrived home to discover they had split.

For the next few years, my dad and his siblings were shuffled around between family members and friends like a deck of cards. They never knew where they would live or who would care for them while there. During this season of chaos

and instability, my dad's mother moved out to the country
and took my dad, his brother, and his younger sister with her.
One morning, Peggy announced she was going into town and
that she would be home later. That evening came and went
without her return. As did the next morning. And for three
whole days their mother was absent without any communication, leaving the kids to fend for themselves. They had no
phone and little food. My dad tried to make do with what
they had, but they were running out of food. On the third day
of his mother's sudden disappearance, my dad was so upset
he took off walking to go find help. He walked almost ten
miles to a pay phone on the main road and called his father.
Dan immediately responded and rescued them from Peggy's
house. He brought his children to live with him. When they
finally heard from Peggy, they were smothered with a long,
elaborate story. She claimed she was kidnapped by two men
during those three long days. She said they tied her up and
kept her in the back seat of their vehicle. Her explanation
seemed full of weak excuses and unnecessary justification. This
began a new norm for my dad. His mother would continue
to wander in and out of his life for weeks and even months
at time. Each time she would reappear, her stories became
more far-fetched as she half-heartedly attempted to explain
away her abandonment.

WHEN THE TWO BECAME ONE

It was the summer of my dad's fifteenth year. Like every summer before, he worked at the traveling carnival. One afternoon,
he looked up from his focused work at the cork gun gallery
and across the sea of people gathered for the games and rides.
As he scanned the nameless faces, somewhere between the

Tilt-a-Whirl and the Scrambler, his eyes rested on someone who took his breath away. He couldn't believe it. He hadn't seen her in a while, but there was no mistaking that this was his much-liked former neighbor. She was wearing tight black shorts and a collared button-up shirt. Her medium red hair flowed carelessly down her back. Of course, it was my mom. In that instant, my dad made a silent vow to himself that he would never let her go.

My dad and mom wrote letters and tried to bridge the gap between my dad's residence and where my mom lived with her mother. Once a week, my mom undertook the 45-minute trip to spend the day with my dad. They saw each other as much as possible. Their feelings for one another provided the only unchanging factor in either of their lives. Their love grew each day and they soon began talking about getting married after my dad graduated...from high school.

During this season of blossoming love, my dad's mother was absent for quite some time. He didn't even know where she was living. But one cool morning, Peggy showed up at their house unannounced. She was living in Houston and wanted my dad and his sister to come back with her. Freddie and Lana were not very fond of the idea of an even longer distance separation. In what was either an attempted reconciliation or just pure manipulation, Peggy presented an interesting offer. She offered to sign for my fifteen-year-old father to marry his girlfriend if they moved to Houston and lived with her.

Doris thought this was a terrible idea! She believed they were too young to get married. So while my mom was old enough to marry without parental consent, she didn't want to hurt her mom by blatantly ignoring her advice. With the appearance of that seemingly unmovable roadblock, my dad moved to Houston while my mom remained with her mother.

However, it didn't take much time for my mom's depression and tears to change her mom's heart on the matter! After watching her daughter weep every single day, Doris finally loaded her on a bus, said goodbye, and sent her to Houston to be with my dad.

Upon arriving in Houston, my mom was horrified. She was clueless about the living conditions before she agreed to the move. Her new residence turned out to be a tiny trailer in which she would live with my dad, his sister, his mother, and his mother's boyfriend. But love is blind and the filthy, cramped quarters did not threaten the joy Lana felt at being reunited with Freddie.

On July 26, 1969, my parents were married in a small church by a pastor who was packing to go on a fishing trip that same day. My dad was newly sixteen, and my mom was nineteen years old. A few family members and friends were present to witness their union. The pastor threw on a suit, gave a brief marriage speech to encourage these strangers, and just like that, two teenagers became husband and wife.

My parents spent the first few months of their marriage trapped in an unfavorable situation. My dad was working a construction job with Peggy's boyfriend. When his paycheck arrived each week, his mother demanded it to help with bills and groceries. My mom found this odd because there was rarely any food in the house. In fact, she would often only eat one meal a day. Thankfully, it wasn't long before both my parents grew weary with the arrangement and decided to take action. My dad called his father, who once again swiftly made the trip to rescue my mom, my dad, and my dad's little sister. This time, my young parents moved in with Doris. My mom was hired for a day job at a cabinet shop while my dad finished high school. He worked in the meat department of a nearby grocery store in the evenings. When they could at last afford a small duplex in the area, they were ecstatic. They finally felt like newlyweds. That is, until they got a knock on their front door after only four months of living alone. My dad's mother and sister were standing on the porch, suitcases in hand. Once again, my parents found themselves sharing a house with extended family. Eventually, Peggy went back to Houston, leaving my dad's sister behind in the care of my parents.

MARRIAGE

According to common standards, statistics, and simple common sense, my parents' marriage really didn't have a prayer. Both brought to the relationship a slew of hurt, pain, rejection, fear, and insecurity. Neither one had a relationship with God. All the odds were stacked against them. They leaned on the fact that, to the extent they could understand the notion, they *loved* each other.

Nearly a year into their marriage, my parents were thrilled to learn they were expecting their first child together. Nine months later, my mom gave birth to my older brother, Eric. He arrived a few months before my Dad graduated high school. Essentially, two teenagers found themselves married with a kid to raise, and they began playing house. As you can imagine, family life was not as glorious as they dreamed it to be. The pressures of marriage, finances, and a new baby took a toll on my parents. They split up before Eric was a year old.

If you thought their story couldn't be more complex or heartbreaking, fasten your seat belts. It gets even crazier.

DATING AROUND

Having both witnessed the tragedy of divorced families, my parents did not want to file for divorce. They always hoped for a different outcome, so instead they decided to date around while remaining married to see if they found someone else they wanted more. If not, they might stay married.

Listen, you and I both know that's a terrible approach, but it made sense to them at the time.

My dad took women on an occasional date here and there, but he wasn't serious about anyone. My mom, however, was heavily pursued by a man named John. She ended up falling in love with John's outgoing and passionate personality. My mom was very honest with John regarding her situation. My mom immediately disclosed that she was still married but was separated from her husband. John revealed that he had already left his wife and was filing for divorce. They seemed to have a mutual understanding of their atypical relationship. John even took my mom to his mother's house one weekend and introduced her to the family as his "girlfriend." After months of dating, they began talking about a possible future together.

But in the months that followed, things began to unravel between my mom and John. My mom discovered that John was not divorcing his wife as he assured her on many occasions. Their relationship was built on a shaky foundation, and it quickly began to crumble.

In the midst of two confusing relationships, my mom tested positive for her second pregnancy. Although completely shocked, she was confident that this baby belonged to her husband, Freddie. (Remember, they were still married and playing house, so they had relations throughout this period of separation.) She had specific reasons for her belief. First and foremost, John was vocal about his possible infertility issues. John was married for nine years, and during that time they never conceived a child. Also, their moments of intimacy were few and far between. My mom had a one-year-old son (my brother) and her twelve-year-old sister-in-law (my dad's sister) still living with her. While the doctor calculated my mom's due date, she performed her own calculations. The conception was traced back to the day my dad brought over divorce papers for my mom to sign. Nostalgia and sadness took over their conversation and one thing led to another. She was certain this was the day their second child was created. After all, it had been weeks since she had been with John. When she delivered her daughter (yours truly) two weeks early, recalculating the conception date didn't cross her mind because her first child also arrived two weeks early.

When my mom first learned of this pregnancy, she approached both men and explained her situation. Freddie was delighted and convinced they should recommit to one another and work on their marriage. On the other hand, John had just learned that his wife was also pregnant. This added to my mom's confidence that I was my dad's biological child. Everyone did what was best in a confusing situation. John reunited with his wife, and she gave birth to a little girl named Wendy Michelle in October. That December, my parents welcomed their daughter, Dana Michelle (that's me!) into the world.

By the following year, my parents were raising two small children, facing life's practical problems, and enduring too many emotional wounds to count. They separated again when I was only a few months old. This time, they eventually divorced. At twenty-one years of age, my dad met and married another young woman in July of 1975. His new wife was only eighteen years old. They became pregnant after a few months of marriage.

LEFT ALONE, BUT NOT REALLY ALONE

My twenty-four-year-old mom was raising two kids on her own. It was not the happily ever-after she so desperately craved. Rejection was a booming voice in her mind and heart and she surrendered to living out its false claims over her life.

She worked as a waitress in clubs. She was able to work late while we were sleeping and was able to be with us during the day. I'm not sure when, or if, she slept. But she determined this was the best situation for our fragmented family since it meant we did not have to grow up being cared for by someone else.

It wasn't long after my parents' divorce that God began to pursue my mom in a mighty way. Ironically, it was my dad's grandmother who convinced her to come to church. Because of my great-grandmother's persistent invitations, my mom began attending church regularly. The more she went, the more she learned about how God's Son died for her sins. And she definitely felt like a sinner. The pressure of working in a club while navigating single motherhood drove her to drink heavily and often. She realized her life was a mess, and she needed a Savior. She accepted Jesus into her heart and life. My mom's eyes were opened, her destiny was changed, and she became a child of God! As God transformed her heart, she prayed continuously for Freddie, the father of her two children, to experience a similar reorientation of heart toward the Lord.

While my mom was living in renewal and redemption, my dad and his new wife welcomed their daughter, Shawna Lynn, June 23, 1976. Adding a newborn to an already unstable marriage proved too much for my dad and his second wife. These two lost and wounded people were trying to make a marriage work while enduring the difficulties of a new baby. It was a recipe for disaster. Their marriage deteriorated before they celebrated their second wedding anniversary.

My dad and mom began to talk again. They reunited in friendship. It only took a few invitations before my dad agreed to attend church with my mom. My dad's life was just as much of a train wreck as my mom's when she first attended church. He was only twenty-four years old, twice divorced, with three children. He saw something different and appealing in my mom's new life. He wanted whatever she had. He realized he too needed a Savior and accepted Jesus into his heart and life. His eternity in heaven was set in stone! My mom's prayers bore the sweetest fruit.

As the natural progression of events would have it, my parents remarried on November 18, 1977. I was the four-year-old flower girl and my brother, Eric, was the six-year-old ring bearer! It's amazing how God produces beauty from ashes! It would be wonderful to wrap up our story right here, to tell you that we all finally lived the life we always wanted. But life is not simple, and our endurance, commitment, and reliance upon the Lord would be further tested down the road.

WHAT MATTERS

Rejection, neglect, and abandonment are harsh realities for so many people! I'm certain that at some point in our lives, we can all say we have felt rejected by someone or neglected in a situation or relationship. My parents' situation was obviously on the extreme end of the spectrum. My mom went from living amongst violent abuse to being abandoned on a daily basis. The safe and stable rug of a unified family was ripped out from beneath my dad's feet, never to return again. Both childhood experiences were shocking and damaging.

All of us can pinpoint our experiences somewhere on the sliding scale of Rejection. Life is hard. We are constantly susceptible to being wounded by others. Hurt people hurt other people. Because of the Jesus in my parents, they were both able to forgive their own parents and cultivate a relationship with them until they all passed away. I had relationship with all of them as well. Most of my grandparents, if not all, met and accepted Jesus, so I witnessed completely different people than those who raised my parents.

FIND THE ROOT

Each of us has felt hopeless. Think of a time when the odds felt stacked against you. How did God see you through? If you are still in that season, try admitting you need the Lord and take His hand while His unconditional love helps you stand. God is a big God and is for you, even if He seems absent.

Sometimes love can redeem a lot of brokenness. In what area of your life have you chosen to love when all else seemed unobtainable, unsure, and unstable? Reflect with thankfulness on how love helped cover things.

Abuse is never acceptable. If you find yourself in an abusive situation, now is the time to get help. Get out and get help. Now. Put down my book. You are worth so much more and deserve to be treated as such! The National Domestic Violence contacts are: 1-800-799-7233, 1-800-787-3224, or thehotline.org.

My parents' journey offered them several opportunities to forgive people who hurt them. Forgiveness is actually a gift to yourself! It doesn't excuse what the other person did to you; rather, it frees you from a lifetime of bitterness toward them. Dwelling in bitterness is like drinking poison and expecting the other person to die. It doesn't happen. It only makes you sicker. Ask God if there is anyone you need to forgive in order to free yourself. Choosing forgiveness always brings healing.

Chapter Two

GROWING PAINS

MY EARLY YEARS

I do not remember my earliest years when things were so chaotic with my parents. I was just a baby. I do, however, have memories of when they were divorced and my dad married a different woman. Because my parents shared custody, my brother and I stayed with my dad and his new wife on the weekends. Sometimes I can still envision the floor plan of their small house. As memories would have it, sometimes we remember the bad more than the good. I did not like going to their house. My new step-mom was only a teenager. She, like my dad, came from intense chaos and brought as much baggage as he did into the relationship. She was a wounded little girl herself, and she was in no position to be a wife and mom to two stepchildren.

My brother and I sometimes had accidents while we slept. This angered our step-mom. She either made us change our own sheets or threatened to make us take a pacifier, because "babies need pacifiers" and "babies wet the bed." Understandably, my brother and I were very relieved when we no longer required to spend time there. Years after their divorce, my dad's ex-wife also accepted Jesus as her Savior. She then became an extension of our family, often joining us for holidays and celebrations. There is redemption available to all.

Naturally, I was happy when my parents remarried, although I probably did not grasp the immense value of it at that time. From then on, I had a fairly normal childhood, according to my definition of "normal" in the '80s. I lived an average life—not boring, but not overflowing with drama or excitement. Even though my parents didn't have an incredible marriage, I knew they were finally stuck together for life. It brought me a peace I never knew before, a confidence that they would never split up again. I had a brother. I had a sister who lived with us on the weekends. Life was good.

Something I always admired about my mom was her ability to love a stepchild as her own. She always emphasized that we don't say "half" or "step," because family is family. Often times, rejected people end up rejecting others. Although Rejection had barged into my mother's life from a very early age, she didn't let it determine how she treated others. It is a beautiful expression of who my mom is on the inside. Blood did not matter here. Shawna was her husband's daughter, and therefore her daughter, too. In fact, if she was ever asked how many children she had, her answer was a quick and emphatic, "Three!"

Growing up, I was irritated when people would question our family situation. My sister lived with her mother during the week, so she didn't attend school with me. There were a few seasons she decided she wanted to live with us full time, but for the most part, we only spent time with her on the weekends. It wasn't uncommon for people to ask me about her, as they tried to decipher our family situation. I said what my mom always modeled, "She is my *sister*." End of story.

We moved several times throughout my upbringing, which proved to be the most trying for me. My parents constantly struggled to make ends meet. They would sign a lease for a rental house, only to sign for a new place six months later in an attempt to save money. For a short season, we moved in with my mom's brother, his wife, and their new baby. During my fourth grade year, we moved a total of four times, forcing me to attend four different schools in one year. I was "the new girl" *four times in one year*. It obviously took a toll on me, because I developed constant debilitating headaches.

One area we moved to was not far from where my parents first met. The area was heavily populated with Spanish-speaking people. I only spoke English. At my new school, it was painfully evident I was in the minority. The extreme stress caused my headaches to become more frequent. I was absent for a significant number of days during my short time there. Honestly, I sometimes faked headaches to avoid stepping foot in the school where I felt like such an outcast. I did not fit in.

Eventually, my parents took me to the doctor, and I was admitted to the hospital to undergo a series of tests. I did not know it at the time, but they suspected a brain tumor. Thankfully, it was just good old fashion migraines! During my fifth grade year, we finally planted our roots in Arlington for good. To this day, my parents still live in that house. I love that house. It is a place I will always walk into feeling safe and at home.

Our family went to church nearly every time the doors were open: Sunday mornings, Sunday nights (some of you may remember those days), Tuesday visitation, Wednesday choir, and Acteens (a group for young girls to learn about missions). I think I was as close as it comes to a professional church attendee. I liked going to church. It was a safe place for me. I knew everyone, and everyone knew me. Looking back, I realize our church possessed something unique that so many churches lack today. We were a family. We were a community. We were a culture. If someone was missing, we knew. I still maintain many relationships from my early childhood at that church. We've enjoyed Youth Group reunions, and we are all in agreement: after attending many different churches in our adulthood, we cultivated something truly special in our childhood church.

MY BUB

While my later years as a child were mostly stable and joyful, my teen years brought with them pain, heartbreak, and an enormous amount of stress, all of which related to my older brother. Eric was one of the most unique people on the planet. He was incredibly gifted in many areas. First of all, he was gorgeous. He had dimples that melted many girls' hearts. Second, he was an artist and an incredible poet. Oh! And he could *dance*!

But sometime during his early teen years, his life began to spiral out of control, although his struggle was subtle at first. Growing up in Arlington, an area known for its "rich and snobby people," was not easy for us average folk. Like me, I think Eric wrestled with fitting in and figuring out where he belonged. Artists and creative people tend to be deep thinkers by nature, and my Bub was always thinking. By junior high, he figured out what peer groups *weren't* for him, but he was still trying to decide *who* he was.

Music affected him greatly. I could be unfamiliar with a song's lyrics but still seem to sing along. I wasn't afraid of making up my own words. Not my Bub. He knew every line of every song! He listened to innumerable songs and albums over and over. But I noticed a change in him as he began to listen to edgier music. It started with Duran Duran and Depeche Mode, then he moved on to Def Leopard and Guns N' Roses. The progression continued as his interest shifted to groups like Twisted Sister, Violent Femmes, and Suicidal Tendencies. The band names alone speak volumes of their messages.

I think it was during the Duran Duran days when he finally reached the conclusion about the person he was and the person he wanted to be. He decided to shave his hair, and with that he became one of the first "New Wavers" in Arlington. This definitely grabbed the attention of many. I don't know if any of us were prepared for the kind of attention he would draw. Most of the girls found him sexy and intriguing. The guys, on the other hand, were awful to him. Unjustifiable insults like "queer" and "faggot" were hurled at him often. The guys at our school threatened regular beatings, and sometimes followed through with them. My Bub was a gentle giant. He never made fun of or hurt anyone. Unfortunately, he became an easy target simply because of the way he wore his hair. And let's be honest, I'm certain the guys were jealous of all the unending attention he was getting from the girls.

During this year, I watched my Bub's internal struggle manifest physically. He tasted alcohol for the first time when he was about fifteen years old. He was at a friend's house, and they broke into the dad's liquor cabinet. When my Bub came home that night, he was completely drunk. This seemingly innocent misbehavior was the catalyst for a lifetime of addiction. He preferred a numbed reality to *actual* reality. I was in the seventh grade. From that point on, I volunteered myself as his protector. Even though he was older, his addiction seemed to stunt him emotionally and psychologically. I think he appreciated it when I came to his rescue when he was actually in need. However, he found my over-protective tendencies to be a little annoying at times and I probably embarrassed him in front of his friends. He didn't always receive my unwarranted protection well. But he knew how much I adored him!

What had been a slow alternation of his character accelerated when my Bub was in high school. My family was always in need of more space in our three-bedroom home. My parents decided to take in half the garage and build a bedroom for my Bub. They even let him paint murals on his wall—an artist's dream come true! He let his creative gifts flow with freedom as he painted every wall and even his door. Word about his room, that he nicknamed "The Forrest," spread across town. A reporter from the local newspaper called to see what the fuss was about. He came to our house for pictures of the artwork and interviewed Eric. My Bub and his room were featured in a large article in the newspaper! By this time, his physical appearance became darker. He shaved and spiked his hair more dramatically and wore black eye-liner. The darkness he was dabbling in started to become his reality. The darker the music, the darker he dressed, and the more he drank.

It wasn't unusual for me to receive a phone call from a stranger, informing me that my Bub needed a ride home from a party because he was too drunk to drive. I was only known as "Eric's little sister." I don't think his friends even knew my name. But I was not quiet like my Bub. I did not have a problem silencing bullies. I would not hesitate to breakup fights when guys were attempting to harass my drunk brother. I could not tolerate bullying, especially when directed toward my sweet Bub.

One night, I was called to come fetch my brother at a local bar and grill. I pulled up to the front to see my Bub standing near the curb with a so-called "friend." He was so drunk he didn't even recognize me. His face was totally blank, numb, and cold. His friend helped him into the front seat. It was the first time I'd seen a person so drunk they looked lucky to be alive. On the car ride home, Eric slurred cruel insults at me:

"You think you are all that!"

"You are a goody-two shoes."

While I don't remember every exact word, I know his declarations about me were scattered with many swear words. I knew he was just trying to hurt me. I think he resented the fact that I didn't cause much trouble at the time. I said, "Stop! You don't mean this and tomorrow you will feel bad or won't even remember." I got him home and helped him to his room, but not before I found his keys and hid them in my own room.

For better or worse, my parents were completely unaware of what was going on under their own roof. They always went to bed right after the ten o'clock news. They both worked physically taxing jobs and they required an adequate amount of sleep each night. As the enemy would have it, so much darkness took place in our home while my parents slept peacefully. There is no blame or shame that should be placed on my parents; we were teenagers doing teenager things when our parents went to bed. My Bub acted up, and I protected him. This senseless formula became our norm.

Growing up with an alcoholic father positioned my mom to be against alcohol in her adulthood. She did not want it in her house at all. Period. Naturally, Bub found ways to hide it in his room, going so far as to cut a hole in the wall behind his bed. I can recall many school nights he spent drinking with friends in his room. I marched right into his room and yelled at them. I shook my finger and firmly told his friends, "My mom does not want alcohol in her house! So stop bringing it over!" Irritated, they would grab their liquor and leave while I endured my brother's anger over ending his little party.

I made it a habit to go into Eric's room and search for his keys. My brother's favorite thing to do while he was drunk was to take a drive. I knew this, so as the "protector," I tried to be the keeper of his keys. Sometimes my Bub would turn them over without a problem, but other times it would be a struggle. Occasionally he would grab the keys, march out the door, get in his car, and leave. All the while I would beg God to let him be in his bed in the morning.

It wasn't uncommon for me to receive an apology note from my Bub the day after an incident. On the few occasions my parents left town, my Bub seized the opportunity to live it up and throw a party! One time, I walked into a house filled with wasted teenagers. I was overwhelmed by the smell of rubbing alcohol, which I would later discover to be from a drug called Ether. The house was a disaster. There were beer cans, liquor bottles, and spills all over the place. People were everywhere. There was one person passed out in the middle of our living room floor. She had inhaled a little too much of that drug they were passing around. I went nuts! It didn't take long for news to spread that the party was over because Eric's little sister was home. The next morning I woke up to a clean house and a note that read: Sis—I'm at work. I cleaned up, *loaded the dishwasher, and mopped the floors. I'm really sorry. I love you, Bub.* I teared up and rolled my eyes at the same time.

I knew he meant it. I also knew it would happen again.

ME

I owe a lot to my mom for her honesty throughout my life, even though she could be *too* honest at times. But when it came time for the story of my conception, I was glad she held nothing back. By the time I learned about the birds and the bees, more questions began to stir in my thirteen-year-old mind. One morning, I was getting ready for the day in the small dressing area between my parents' bedroom and bathroom. It had a big mirror and countertop where I stood to do my hair. I would blow dry my bangs while applying hairspray and makeup: blue eye shadow and navy eyeliner. This particular day, while my mom stood in her bedroom, I asked out of the blue, "Mom, if you were with Dad and John around the time I was conceived, how do you know for *sure* I am Dad's kid?"

Her response was quick and without hesitation, "I just know. I know the day you were conceived. I'm just certain."

She proceeded to tell me about the time my dad delivered divorce papers to her house. Emotional nostalgia served as a catalyst for their physical reunion, for what they thought was one last time. I'm sure I was grossed out by this story on some level, but for whatever reason, her answer was good enough for me. At least for that time.

At school, I was pretty well-liked. I had a lot of friends and not too many enemies. My biggest hindrance was my smart mouth. I often offended people. I was not afraid to speak up about situations I found unjust or wrong. I developed a sharp, bold tongue, partly as a defense mechanism. After taking the "StrengthsFinders" test a few years ago, I discovered one of my top strengths is communication. Upon this discovery, my mind immediately shifted back to my adolescent years. Any strength we have not submitted to the Lord, the enemy will twist and use for his schemes. The Lord had plans for me to learn healthy communication for His glory. But for a while, my untamed tongue would communicate ugly things to hurt people. Thankfully, it usually seemed to blow over as quickly as it blew out of my mouth.

Although my friends were many in quantity, I remember having an inconsolable feeling that I did not fit in. Living in an affluent part of Arlington added salt to this wound. We were never rich. My parents did their best to help me keep up with the trendy clothes and belongings. Every day, girls would come to school with $200 leather Dooney and Bourke purses hanging from their arms. I thought my life was over if I did not get a Dooney purse. Clearly, I was crushed under the high pressure of the standards in my community. Eventually, I was able to purchase a beloved designer bag I found for half price—only $50! But it was the canvas kind. It was not leather like everyone else's bags. That's how much of my life felt during this season—close, but not quite enough.

If the handbag stress wasn't enough, I consistently kept a calendar detailing the outfits I wore in order to avoid wearing repeated outfits too often. It sounds like a joke, but the friends whose company I kept would not hesitate to ask, "Didn't you wear that shirt last week?" I was surrounded by girls who rarely wore the same outfit twice. The fact that we had less money than everyone else around us was never hidden. My feelings of inferiority and inadequacy increased. Because of this obvious split in economic status, and perhaps more so because of my wild insecurity about it, I was very unsure in my friendships at school. I never knew who my true friends were, or if I had even one. There were times I had a few best friends at school. Then something would happen, and we would have a friendship "breakup." Those were painful and left deep scars on my young heart.

My church friends were pretty solid, and I felt more secure in those relationships. Community was a huge reason I gravitated toward church involvement. But even those friendships couldn't completely save me from the rejection and instability I experienced in my relational encounters at school.

School friendship circles always brought out severe self-doubt. After moving so much in my earlier years, I desperately wanted to establish friendships and *belong* somewhere. From fifth grade until high school, I was a part of what was probably considered the "popular group." I came to this decision through the process of elimination as I figured out in which groups I did *not* belong. I wasn't what was known as a "roper" (cowgirl), "nerd" (super intellectual), "freak" (heavy metal druggie), or "new waver" (like my Bub). Of course, although I hung out in the popular group, I never *felt* popular. I constantly felt I didn't *really* belong in that group. Instead, I felt like an outsider with no place to call home.

I sought friendships through my track team, but I seemed to meet dead ends in that arena as well. I was a very fast runner and ran track for years. I won many races, earning stacks of ribbons. My sophomore year, I was the only one in my class who qualified for the varsity team. My relay team even ended up qualifying for the regional competition. However, my insecurity overwhelmed my cultivated confidence around my junior and senior teammates. I let our age difference create a canyon instead of allowing my proven abilities build a bridge of friendship.

Although my desire for affirmation from friends at school and those on my track team consumed most of my thoughts, nothing drove my actions and decisions as much as my desire to be accepted by boys. And nothing stung as badly as when I was rejected by them. "Rejection" became personified as it appeared to have a strong opinion about my life when it came to the fellas. I was boy crazy. It seemed that I liked or even "loved" a new guy every other day. At the time, it just appeared normal. Nothing to be concerned about. I was just a cute girl who was learning to *appreciate* cute boys.

Knowing what I know now, I realize I was trying to fill a void in my heart concerning males. When girls experience a healthy father-daughter relationship, it sets a precedent for their interactions with other men. It helps them establish a solid grid concerning their future relationships. It also minimizes the feeling that you "need a guy" in order to be happy. I did not begin my fascination with boys armed with this healthy set of standards. Although my dad was a good and loving father, I don't recall having much of a relationship with him until I was older.

I found myself looking to boys to fulfill a need I didn't know I had. I had my first real boyfriend when I was a junior in high school. I was seventeen years old. That relationship proved to be a very bad example of what a relationship should look like. It was full of hot-tempered fights and heated arguments. Thankfully, we didn't drag it out too long and only dated for about five months. The first day of my senior year brought with it the first of what would be a series of painful heartbreaks. That evening, there was a fun event planned to kick off the school year. My boyfriend asked me to go with him, but I already made plans to go with my best friend, Chrystal. He was not pleased with this arrangement. He wanted to show up to the first event of his senior year with his girlfriend on his arm. Instead, he showed up with some guy friends and ignored me the entire evening. Later that night, he called me and mumbled something about being proud I was his girlfriend, but disappointed I picked my friends over him. Then the words came. "I want to breakup." This was not the start I dreamed for my glorious senior year! Rejection showed up on the first day of what should have been the best year of my life—graduation year.

But as teenagers do, I seemed to get over my broken heart sooner than I anticipated. Someone else caught my attention. Brad started out as an innocent study partner. But it wasn't long until we stopped studying school material and started studying each other. He asked me to "go with him," as we called it in 1990. He was a really sweet guy, a classic high school sweetheart. It was the best relationship I ever had until I met my husband. It was the first time I uttered the phrase "I love you" to anyone other than family and friends. We were really involved with church. We attended weekly Young Life functions. We participated in a more intimate Bible study group called Campaigners. We were best friends with other couples, and it was a really sweet relationship. We did fight, but it was mostly my fault. Our fights always stemmed from my insecurities. I either wanted more time with him or accused him of spending all his time on the baseball field. He wasn't a perfect guy, but he was devoted to me.

Once we graduated from high school, he moved away to play baseball for a junior college in Waco. It was only an hour and a half away. We thought the distance would work because we weren't that far away from each other. I would make the trip every chance I had, sometimes arriving in an hour. Brad's baseball schedule kept him busy, and he wasn't able to come home very often. After our second semester at separate colleges, he decided our long distance relationship wasn't working. He couldn't come home enough, and he was frustrated I couldn't come there enough. A week before Valentine's Day, he broke up with me. Mercifully, it was sweeter than my previous breakup. He actually drove the 90 miles to say it to my face. We held each other and wept for what felt like hours. We were both very sad that life was taking us in different directions.

Life proved to take him in a new direction faster than I expected. He found a new girlfriend on campus within a couple of weeks. I called him one night, probably hoping he changed his mind, and he acted very cold. He eventually admitted he had met someone else. I suspected this other girl was a major factor in our breakup. Being dumped was painful, but being *replaced* seemed worse. Rejection saw this as a perfect opportunity to reinforce the lie that not only was I unwanted, but easily replaceable.

WHAT MATTERS

Life can feel so unstable and unpredictable. It is especially hard when you are in situations you cannot control. Growing up, I found myself in a lot of those situations. I didn't have influence over my parents moving so often or having an addict for a brother.

Sometimes the only variable is how we respond to the deck of cards we are dealt. We can chose joy, even when things don't make us feel happy. We can rest in God's peace even when things are far from peaceful. When situations are not necessarily changeable, our attitudes always have room for a little adjustment! Even when we are rejected, we can chose to accept and break the cycle of pain.

FIND THE ROOT

We live in a world full of step and half family members. The harsh reality is most of us have been touched by divorce in some way. Is there a new family member you need to choose to love? Accepting, instead of rejecting, will always bear sweeter fruit.

Living with an addict is one of the toughest and most stressful situations! You love the person and see such potential in their future. They can hurt you, disappoint you, lie to you, steal from you, and curse at you. Then they apologize and give you false hope. And repeat. It's exhausting. Ask God for wisdom. Some of us need to remove an addict from our lives (until they are clean). Some of us are enabling an addict and the Lord can't work until we relinquish control. Don't let the enemy rob you of a fulfilling life just because you love an addict. Jesus is their only Savior! Alcoholics Anonymous is a great resource for family and friends of addicts. Support groups like this recognize that friends and families of addicts often need emotional support along with the addict.

When earthly relationships lack anything, there is a heavenly relationship that never lacks. A personal relationship with God Almighty can make up for any human lack. If you find yourself feeling like you need a man like I did, ask God to fill the empty spots in your heart. Focusing on God will always be more fulfilling and His words never return void.

Chapter Three

I DO...I MEAN, I DON'T

At the tender age of twenty-one, I experienced, in my opinion, the worst rejection a young girl could ever experience.

I was in a relationship with someone for almost three years. Jason and I grew up together at church, but he wasn't heavily involved. In our teen years, he was known around town as a wild guy, a loose cannon who drove too fast and partied too much. But somewhere around the age of twenty, he entered the Marines and cleaned up his life. He began attending church consistently. We were both very involved in the college group. The Lord softened Jason, and in turn, he became very attractive to me. His training as a Marine showed in his physique, he maintained his charm as life of the party, and now he passionately loved the Lord! He asked me out, and so we began our lengthy relationship. We were two very outgoing people with major zests for life. When things were good, they were great; when things were bad, they were *horrible*. In this relationship, Rejection constructed a breeding ground in my heart.

Jason's family owned a farm house located a little over two hours away from where we lived. We spent many weekends there together. We would go with his family or take a group of friends. I have a lot of fond memories from that place.

One weekend we had plans to spend a few days at The Farm with his whole family, an activity that was happily a part of our routine by this point. But just before we were scheduled to leave, Jason got mad at me for something. It was quite possible he had a very good reason. However, his response was unhealthy and he delivered a harsh punishment. Instead of loading my bags in his car, he left me on my front porch and headed to The Farm for the weekend without me. I was wrecked. I fell on the floor of my bedroom and let out a moan of sheer devastation. He abandoned me. For someone who struggles with Rejection, being left behind was a particularly heinous blow. My mother held me and tried to comfort me, but there was nothing she could do. I felt like the most unloved and unwanted girl on the planet. It was the longest, loneliest, coldest weekend. Because I was very (stupidly) forgiving, I forgave my boyfriend when he returned home. He said what I needed to hear and gave me assurance he would not repeat the offense. But Rejection planted a host of seeds in my heart that weekend, and they took deep root. During the remainder of that relationship, those seeds received continual watering.

To my shock, Jason repeated the same stunt a few months later. Something angered him once again, and once again he took off to The Farm without me! History was repeated as I stood amongst my packed bags with my jaw dropped and my heart shattered on the floor. I was horrified that he could abandon me again, knowing how much pain it caused before.

I was insecure and controlling. I didn't usually *do* anything *mean*. But my insecurities left him feeling smothered and controlled. In turn, he felt the need to escape me often. It was a vicious cycle. I wanted to be loved, pursued, desired, and cherished. But my unhealthy, broken soul overcompensated and became clingy. So Jason would run off or blow up, or both. But this particular time he left me, my mom said, "Not again! You aren't leaving my daughter all weekend on the floor of her bedroom with a mangled heart. Come get her!" To his credit, he agreed to turn around and meet us in the middle of the route. They passed me off like a baton. Bizarrely, I was better in an instant and forgave him immediately. I was at The Farm with the man I *loved*. All seemed to be right again.

Our relationship became steadier. At twenty-one and twenty-three we attended college together at Dallas Baptist University. I was studying to be a teacher, with graduation just three semesters away. He was studying business with only one year until graduation. We really had no business getting married, but in our immature and unhealthy minds, it seemed like the next logical step. I *may* have pressured him a little, as I desired permanence. After all, our relationship *had* improved. We were in a good season with less fighting.

Romantically, he asked me to marry him at The Farm!. With tears streaming down my face, I enthusiastically said, "Yes!" I do not recall the exact date, but it was sometime in the fall of 1994. Nevertheless, it was the happiest time of my life. It appeared I would never have a broken heart over a broken relationship again.

All of our parents joyfully assisted in the proposal. They were at The Farm waiting to congratulate us, even his father. My fiancé's mother loved and accepted me over the years, but his father often made his disapproval known. This offered Rejection another opportunity to remind me that I wasn't accepted. Even though I won Jason's mother's loving approval,

I longed for his father's approval as well. Oh, what a father's love can do! He wanted the best for his son, understandably so. Unfortunately, his disapproval inflicted more wounds upon an already injured young woman. Regardless, nothing from the past mattered once his son proposed, because I finally gained his acceptance. I floated on air as he proudly introduced me to his friends and colleagues as his "future daughter." It was the approval my heart so desperately needed.

HAPPILY EVER AFTER?

The following six months were bustling with wedding plans. I viewed everything through the glorious lens of engagement bliss. Things were going very well. The biggest obstacle we faced was, as usual, money. My parents struggled to earn every penny they could in order to pay for the wedding. My mother's father blessed us with money to make up for where they lacked. The wedding was paid in full. The dress and decor were purchased. The bridesmaids' dresses were being sewed. The invitations were addressed. We were just anticipating the arrival of July 29, the day we would become husband and wife.

May 17, 1995, marked a major event on the timeline of my life. It altered the course of my life. My fiancé went away for a guys' weekend at The Farm. While he was there, we had a disagreement on the phone. It took place in a room full of his young, single guy friends. I imagine they made fun of his ball and chain back home. Upon his return, he acted strange as we walked upstairs to his bedroom. He sat, visibly overwhelmed, in the chair at his desk. He wasted no time as he aloofly stuttered, "I…I am just not ready. I am not ready to do this."

Totally confused, I questioned, "Ready to do what?"

His answer was emotionless, "I am not ready to settle down and get married."

His tone was the same as if he had changed his mind about a movie he wanted to see. I froze in total dismay, unsure if my ears were working correctly. To add insult to injury, he said, "In fact, I don't want to be with you anymore. I want to breakup."

I was blindsided and utterly devastated. I never saw any signs he wanted to change his mind after a six-month engagement. None. A month prior, he actually asked if we could move the wedding date up, as he was anxious to marry me. If he battled doubts, he never once expressed them to me until that moment. The bomb exploded and completely shattered my heart into a million pieces. I was sitting somewhere near his window at the foot of his bed. I collapsed on the floor, as his decisions so often led me to do. I begged him to change his mind. I was convinced he had gone temporarily insane. I was in a state of sheer shock and panic. He remained cold and unmoving. He remained glued to his chair and extended no comfort as I unraveled before his eyes. It was evident he was distressed, but not for me, only for himself. He wanted to end our relationship, and now he was just trying to survive the fallout. Without an ounce of tenderness, he kicked me to the curb.

In that moment, Rejection was no longer satisfied by only small bites of my heart. It swallowed me whole.

THE AFTERMATH

At twenty-one years old, I was left with the task of un-planning a wedding. I was dumped by the man I loved. Three years of building a relationship was undone with a single swift, demolishing decision. But you can't just plan a wedding, decide you don't want it, and walk away. There was a massive list of things to be canceled. I thought about the many gifts I'd received at my wedding shower just the week before. I certainly couldn't keep them. Humiliating! My mother called each of her friends. Every single woman said, "Tell her to take it back and use the money to get something she wants!" (bless them). No one wanted their gifts back. Boldly, my ex-fiancé asked if he could acquire some of the store credit. I am certain my answer contained explicit language. I reminded him about the large sum of (nonrefundable) money my parents contributed for our wedding. This not only caused a huge blow to my heart, but also a huge blow to my parents' pocketbook.

I did insist he share some of the responsibilities. To his credit, he agreed and helped me cancel a few things. Since he had placed the diamond ring on my finger, I insisted he take it off my finger. He said he didn't want the ring back. He was probably being kind, but I took him up on the offer. I was not going to let him off easily! I thought about selling it to repay my parents for some of the money they lost. Part of me hoped he would want to put it back on my finger.

Since our pastor was already planning to marry us, I thought it would only be appropriate to inform him of our split face-to-face. I wanted my ex-fiancé to face the music. I also secretly hoped he may change his mind in the process. He agreed we should talk to the pastor. Jason was a decent guy, after all. He also was dealing with his own heartache, confusion, and major life alteration. We arrived at the church at the same time for our meeting with the pastor. The pastor called my ex-fiancé into his office first. They were in there for a while. I sat on the couch in the waiting room, doubled over with a sick stomach. A part of me, the broken part, wished the pastor would talk some sense into him and encourage him to reunite with me.

I just wanted the pain to stop.

After what seemed like hours, the door finally opened and my ex-fiancé walked out, motioning for me to enter the room. I walked into the room and nervously sat down on the couch across from my pastor. I don't know what I was expecting him to say, but he didn't say what I had hoped. He leaned toward me with kindheartedness. After all, he's known me since I was an infant, and he performed the re-marriage of my parents. His voice was thick with compassion as he delivered a hard truth, "Sugar, this guy is not ready to be married! In fact, he has no business being in a relationship. Run. Run! Don't turn back!"

I collected the shattered pieces of my heart, rose from the couch, and hopelessly walked out of the church. Whatever Jason confessed to our pastor was enough for my pastor to prompt me to pursue anything but the revival of that relationship.

My heartache was so deep I would physically hurt from the pain. My knotted and queasy stomach repelled food. I wanted my life to end rather than to deal with the devastating grief. I wasn't suicidal, I just wanted out of my own life and my own skin. I couldn't see past my own ache. It is very similar to the grief of actually losing someone to death. Not only did I think he was my future husband, but my life was so intertwined with his. I had grown to not only love him, but I liked him. We spent so many holidays, vacations, and weekends together. We shared almost three years of endless memories together. Now, I had to accept the fact that he didn't want to share another memory with me. I no longer had him in my life all at. It all happened in an instant. It was too much, too fast. People offered sympathy, but no one really understood the unique kind of suffering I was enduring.

SEARCHING FOR SOLACE

The broken engagement caused me to question everything I thought to be true. I was still convinced Jason made a mistake. I thought *he* was the one I was supposed to marry. His mistake was ruining my life, and I couldn't reconcile that in my mind and heart. It seemed too tragic and unfair. I cried out to God on so many occasions, begging Him to change Jason's mind.

As the Lord drew me into His presence, I found comfort in reading the Bible. In the aftermath of my heartbreak, I struggled to sleep. If I didn't fall asleep crying, I woke up in the middle of the night crying. When I opened my eyes in the morning, I felt my bare ring finger. I reminded myself that this wasn't a nightmare; this was my real life. So at night, I lit a candle, sprawled on my floor, and opened my Bible to the Psalms. I read. I cried. I prayed. Read. Cried harder. Prayed. I was a mangled mess of a girl. My pink leather Bible became saturated with my tears. I filled it with underlines and highlights. I found it comforting to read about David in the Psalms. He spoke like a mighty man in one verse, and in the next verse cried, "God, where are you? Why have you left me?"

I held fast to Psalm 34:18: "The Lord is close to the brokenhearted and saves those who are crushed in spirit."

It gave me enormous peace because I was the definition of one brokenhearted and crushed in spirit! I needed to feel God close because I never felt so alone. I read until I was so sleepy that my body's only option was to give in to the fatigue. I became so dependent on God's Word to get me through my long days and lonely nights.

The split and the grief that followed seemed like an unending road paved with thorns. My relationships with Jesus, my family, and my friends kept me from a complete emotional breakdown. From early elementary school, God blessed me with some very amazing mentors at my church. There were three specific women who I called my "Other Mothers." I like to think I was just blessed with these women. But with my strong personality and iron will, it was possible God knew I needed an army of women to surround me. These women were strategically crucial during different seasons of my life. In this particular trial, I found comfort at their homes. It was very difficult for me to be at my own house during these months. Just a few weeks earlier, my house was brimming with anticipation. My wedding dress hung in my closet, wedding invitations were scattered across my floor, and bridal magazines were displayed on my dresser. Now my home represented something radically different: I still lived with my parents, I wasn't planning a wedding anymore, and I was alone. I found it too painful to face this constant reminder, so most days, I left. I hid in the homes of my "Other Mothers." I shed buckets of tears on their couches and at their kitchen tables.

FOOL ME ONCE, FOOL ME TWICE

A few months after we broke up, I received a call from my ex-fiancé. He was in my driveway and asked me to come outside. It alarmed me because this was the first time I had contact with him since the day we met with our pastor. My initial response was, "Why? Are you going to hurt me?"

He answered, "No! I just want to talk to you."

I apprehensively walked outside to his car. I opened the door, and he asked me to get in so we could talk. Immediately upon sitting in the front seat, I could smell the alcohol. We talked for a few hours. In that conversation, he told me how miserable he was feeling. Strangely, hearing that brought me comfort. He was so cold and emotionless during our breakup, it appeared he felt nothing. His outward regret finally proved he cared a little. He admitted he'd been drinking to numb his pain. He questioned if he made a mistake in ending our relationship. There was that side of me that wanted to say, "*See, I told you!*" The other side of me thought the alcohol made him extra chatty and nostalgic. We left that night agreeing to talk soon.

The following month we entertained an undefinable relationship. Communication between us was kept secret. We only talked when *he* wanted to talk, but my curiosity kept me around anyway. My wounded soul craved the temporary bandage of this uncommitted companionship. Although his motives were immediately questionable, I wondered if the Lord changed Jason's mind. Maybe He was answering my prayers. I was open to *miracles*. But this guy was not the same guy I was about to marry just a few months before. He drank too much and acted annoyingly arrogant. He seemed like the loose cannon I didn't like back in high school. He asked for the ring back, and I wondered if that was the motivation behind his sudden reappearance.

One afternoon, I was upstairs in his bedroom when his desk calendar caught my eye. A girl had written her own name and phone number on the open page. It became clear he had other girls in his life, and evidently in his bedroom. He became more and more unattractive to me.

A few weeks later, I invited him to stop by my house to hang out. He declined. He was getting ready for a day on the lake to jet ski with some friends and didn't have time to see me. A sense of urgency infiltrated my body, and I insisted he come over beforehand. After all, my house was right by the lake, and I assured him it wouldn't take long. He reluctantly agreed. When he arrived, I climbed into the front seat of his car. I wanted clarification and certainty about our relationship. I emphatically told him I refused to continue this weird thing between us.

His quick response was cold and smug, "Fine."

The conversation lasted a total of two minutes. I climbed out of his car for the last time and did not see or talk to Jason again for years.

Even though it was a confusing month, I saw it as a sweet kiss from God. My prayer for Jason's return was answered. And his return convinced me that no mistakes had been made. We were not meant to be together. As a stake in the ground, I hired a jeweler to turn my engagement ring into a necklace. I wore it for years as a symbol, not representing what could have been, but representing what *was* to come in my future. It rested on my chest as a constant reminder and as a promise: I almost married the wrong man, and I would never do that again.

It took me a solid year to feel like I could breathe again. Even though it was a completely different life than I thought I would be living, I finally felt alive again. The painful rejection caused me to question God on more than one occasion. Questions raged when I discovered my ex-fiancé had a serious girlfriend only months after our final separation. I did not feel healthy enough to even consider dating. Remember, *he* was the one who wasn't ready to settle down. So you can imagine my shock when I heard he was getting married. It felt so unfair. Rejection once again roared, reminding me that I was easily replaceable.

WHERE I'M FROM AND WHERE I'M GOING

What stirred me to question my childhood again during this time remains a mystery. I suppose the series of emotions and rejections made me re-examine *everything* about my existence. In the year or two after my engagement ended, I asked my mom some of the same questions I often asked over the years.

The constant questions from people about my looks and height were becoming unbearable. Questions about my height came like rapid fire my whole adult life. It was not only due to the fact that my mom was so short, but that my dad was only 5'9". When I wore heels, I towered over both parents.

My mom was always kind enough to answer anything I asked. She believed in her heart she had nothing to hide. One particular day, I asked if she kept a picture of John. I thought that if I saw a picture, it would give me some sort of gut-feeling about my origin. Maybe I would feel one way or the other. My mom still kept one picture of him. She dug through a little orange box of keepsakes and pulled out a tiny photo.

The photo displayed my mom and John sitting on a park bench together. But this was an old photograph, and the subjects were so small in the photo that I really couldn't decipher much, especially since John was wearing sunglasses. Four things *did* jump out at me as I examined the photo. Although they were sitting down, it was clear my mom was significantly shorter than John. He also looked dark, thin, and dark-headed.

As I stared at the photo, I said softly, "Mom, you never told me he was tall." Conflicting thoughts battled in my mind.

"Why? Do you think you look like him?"

"I can't really tell. But I didn't know he was tall."

I gave the photo back to my Mom, and she tucked it away. The rest of our conversation was irrelevant. I felt content enough to move on in that season of my life. I loved my daddy and was content with him being my daddy. I did, however, mentally catalogue a few facts about the characteristics of John that I had not previously observed: he was tall, thin, dark, and dark-headed. Just like me.

I felt like the Lord gave me the peace I needed to continue living my life without any other questions requiring answers at that time. I still attended church on a regular basis. I grew used to relying on God to get me through anything and everything. After all, the Lord had just proven very faithful during one of the darkest seasons of my life. He never left me or forsook me. I *felt* it.

WHAT MATTERS

Now over twenty years removed, the season after my engagement ended is but a memory. It remains a crucial event on my timeline, of course. It had to happen to get me where I am today. I have been happily married for almost seventeen years only because of Jason's decision. He is happily married now, too! I am thankful for his courage. I cannot imagine the inner stress and turmoil he suffered to make such a monumental, uncomfortable decision. I would not have the husband and the four children I have today if Jason had not set me free. I used to believe he dumped me, but as I matured, I saw that he freed me. He freed me to have the life I now love. So for that, I am forever grateful to him.

FIND THE ROOT

Nothing about rejection is easy. It's the enemy's perfect window to barge in and label you "unloved," "unwanted," or "easily replaceable." If you are broken-hearted, I challenge you to open the Bible. Read. Meditate. God's Word is healing and will speak louder than the enemy's lies. You *are* loved. You *are* wanted. You *are not* replaceable! Rejection is silenced when you truly grasp just how deep and wide God's love is for you!

Try and shift your focus from feeling "dumped" to actually being set free. Trust that God knows best. Even if you think someone's mistake changed the course of your life, find comfort in the fact that God is already working for your good!

Chapter Four

MY TOXIC BEST FRIEND

Rejection and I seemed to be best friends as we never left one another. We went everywhere together. Even though I relied on God during my dark days, I still claimed many unhealed wounds and hurts instead of letting Him heal me. At the time, I didn't possess the knowledge to be freed from those chains. Because of this pain, I lived life viewing everyone and every situation through a distorted lens. I made decisions that perpetually poured salt on these wounds of low self-esteem.

IN ALL THE WRONG PLACES

While I finished up my education degree at Dallas Baptist University, I waited tables at a nearby sports bar. Initially, I was disgusted by the crude behavior of my co-workers. My relationship with the Lord was blossoming, and I was turned off by many of the decisions they made. But over time, as I Corinthians warns, "Bad company corrupts good morals."

It is so true.

It only took six months before I began participating in some of the very things that previously appalled me.

My relationship with God dwindled to nearly nonexistent for a few years in my mid-twenties. I opened the door to the enemy and he made himself comfortable. He didn't have to exert much effort to hinder God's purpose in my life. My behavior encouraged the enemy to do more damage. And I went along with his schemes, blind to my own detriment.

Along with the state of my soul, my relationships progressively declined. I dated off and on during my early twenties. The quality of guys I liked reflected how I felt about myself: lacking due respect. The next serious relationship after my engagement seemed to be the final nail in my emotional coffin.

My best friend from college introduced me to her husband's brother, Jeremy. He was good looking, super outgoing, and everyone liked him. He made his attraction to me obvious, which felt good. His attention toward me made me feel very beautiful! He pursued me like no man ever had before. This flirtation served as a temporary salve on the scars from past rejection, at least at first. It wouldn't take long before more wounds and scars would be inflicted. This relationship progressed quicker than I could have imagined. Watching him fall passionately in love with me was exciting and validating. He wanted to spend most of his days with me. This was great for my insecure, broken soul. We had so much fun together. He could dance and sing, two attributes I always found attractive. Eventually, I realized that not everything was as dreamy as it appeared, but not before I was intertwined in a very sticky web.

The more we were together, the more I calculated the amount of alcohol he consumed. It was alarming! I remember pouring beers out behind his back when he wasn't looking.

Falling back into the old patterns I crafted with my brother, I took on the role of "Protector of the Drunk." I drank socially with him, but it became obvious he had a serious problem. While it didn't take me long to see the red flags, it took me three years to heed their warning.

Over the years, our relationship became volatile. We were volatile. *He* was volatile. We broke up and got back together more times than I can count. After a breakup, he would show up on my doorstep in tears, proclaiming he couldn't live without me. He would promise me the moon and the stars, or that he would get his life back on track for me. He never failed to sweet-talk his way back into my life. I felt so sorry for him, which led me to extend grace. Well, I thought it was grace at the time, but it was really a sick, unhealthy cycle of emotional and psychological abuse.

The dynamics of our relationship continued to spin out of control to the point that fear consumed me. In most cases, I was the one doing the breaking up. It was quite different from being the one dumped. If I'm honest, I kind of liked the control I had over him. It felt better to be in this position than to be the one left behind. Witnessing him beg for my heart again and again made me feel fought for, at first.

But scary things began to happen during our splits. During one time apart, I walked out of my apartment to find flowers left on the windshield of my car. He swore he did not leave them and, in the next breath, accused me of having another boyfriend. In the midst of a different breakup, my phone rang in the middle of the night, waking me from a deep sleep. I answered it, only to hear the person on the other end of the line breathing, speechless. When I traced the calls, I discovered they were made from a pay phone just down the street from my apartment. I lived alone in my apartment, and these pranks caused my paranoia to grow. My tires were slashed two different times during this back and forth, and both times he swore he was not the culprit. I was naive and I believed him the first time. He was very convincing.

MAKING DEALS WITH GOD

In the summer of 1999, a friend and I decided to do a Beth Moore poolside Bible study together. It was in the midst of my longest season of separation from Jeremy. I needed some serious Jesus in my life to bring clarity to my situation. We chose *A Heart Like His*, a study about the life of King David. I hold that summer dear to my heart as it was a significant event on my spiritual timeline. My heart began its biggest change to date. The more I learned about David, the more I understood myself. Mystically, reading David's words in the Psalms helped heal my heart in the twentieth century. David went through serious trials. He was far from perfect. In fact, he was a really good sinner at times. Yet God called him a "man after my own heart" (Acts 13:22). It built my confidence because if anyone felt like a good sinner, it was me! That summer, I realized if God considered someone like David to be so special, He might feel the same about me. It was a tough Bible study that invited me to face some very dark places in my own heart. However, as God's Word never returns void, His Word began to change me. I began to believe in myself again. I began to feel lovable again. I sensed God's redemptive work taking place in my heart and life.

A few months after completing the Bible study, I reconnected with Jeremy. I found he was doing better than ever. He attended church regularly with his family. He quit drinking and partying. He started his own company and worked hard. If I gave him chances when he was not doing *anything* right, why would I not give him a chance when he appeared to be doing *everything* right? I decided it was only fair to try one last time. *Mistake.*

We attended church as part of our weekly routine. Our relationship seemed healthier. It appeared God completed true work in both of our hearts and brought us back together. I wanted to believe that. As the months progressed without any hiccups, we talked about getting married. I'm not sure I believed he was the one. There was a part of me, a part I ignored, that believed this might be my last chance at marriage.

I will never forget the day I sat on the balcony of my apartment alone. I looked up at the sky as I watched beautiful white clouds pass protectively overhead. I whispered to God, "My heart cannot take another broken engagement. I can't have another ring taken off my finger. He is about to ask me to marry him, and I am going to agree. If he is not the one You have for me, please make it clear. Give me a sign *before* he proposes."

Three days later, Jeremy's valiant behavior unraveled in an instant.

It was horrible. Jeremy attended a golf tournament with some friends. In years past, a day on the course was an all-day drinking extravaganza resulting in a very wasted boyfriend. He promised a different outcome this time. He swore he would not touch a drink. Later that day, I called him to chat, and upon hearing his voice, my stomach sank. I knew.

I drove forty-five minutes and waited for him at his house. He eventually made it home and my suspicions were confirmed. He was trashed. And he went nuts! He was furious that I had come to check up on him. He almost rammed my car with his truck as he frantically tried to flee. He jumped a curb, tore off down the street, and left me there. He ignored my calls for the rest of the evening. I didn't even know if he was safe. After hours of worry, I finally tucked myself into bed. Images danced in my head of what might happen as he sped around the city, drunk out of his mind.

Once he sobered up, he agreed to meet me. I looked into his eyes and delivered a promise, "If you ever do something like that again, I will be gone forever." As a stubborn girl, I had the nerve to sit out on my balcony, look up at the same sky and question God. *Again*. I asked, "God, was that your sign? If it was your sign, let it happen again before he proposes."

Less than a week later, knowing the promise I delivered, Jeremy repeated his toxic behavior. He drank too much, he was horrible to me, and things were ugly. I took it as a crystal clear sign. The Lord was showing me that in marrying Jeremy, I would be marrying a severe alcoholic. It was as though a light switched on, or off, whichever way you want to look at it. I realized staying in a relationship with him would be directly disobeying God. My heart was fully closed and finally done with the relationship in an instant. After growing up in the company of an alcoholic, I swore against voluntarily signing up to marry one. I escaped a potential marriage to someone who would have definitely caused me a lifetime of grief, drama, and pain. With my eyes open wide and my mind full of clarity, I broke up with Jeremy for good.

WHAT MATTERS

Okay. Can we just make a deal? Could you please not date the wrong person for a second longer? The only thing worse would be dating them for a minute longer. If something seems off in a relationship or situation, do yourself a favor and get out! That feeling that something is off is most likely the Holy Spirit imparting wisdom to you. Heed it. Run—don't walk— and never look back.

Sometimes certain friendships can be wrong for you, too. Seasons change and so can friendships. You have great worth. Don't remain in a toxic relationship because you're afraid you can't do better, or because you feel like you need to save someone.

FIND THE ROOT

I am assuming most of us have felt guilty or felt like a sinner at some point in our life. Is there an area of your life that you need to let Jesus "clean up" or "clean out?"

Show me your friends and I can predict your future! The company we keep will absolutely influence our life. Choose wisely. Choose people who give life. Choose people who are for you. Choose people who will steer you down a healthy path. Choose people with good morals and character. Ask God if there is a relationship or a season of friendship that needs to end. Obey Him quickly.

Chapter Five

SURRENDER CHANGES EVERYTHING

I ended that relationship in February 2000. That was when I experienced one of the most profound "come to Jesus" moments in my life. My heart, left tattered from previous relationships, continued to fall for the wrong type of guy. Rejection had used my last relationship like a puppet on a string. But God had other plans. Plans to prosper me and not harm me. A few days after I broke up with Jeremy, I came to the end of myself. I was standing in between my bed and my dresser. I fell down on my knees and cried out to God, "I am done. I *will* obey you. I am so tired. I can't fix men."

That day in the bedroom of my apartment, I made a vow to God (one I proudly kept), "The next relationship I have will be with my future husband. I give it to you, God. I commit to wait for the one you have for me."

That was the moment of my true surrender to God. At five years, old I knew Jesus was real. I knew He loved me and I, in return, gave my heart to Him. But I never truly surrendered my will to Him until this point. After I handed my sorrows and worries to the Lord, I felt a rush of peace infiltrate my soul. For the first time, I rested in the hands of God. I gave Him complete control of my life, and the one Mighty King who had the power to rock my world, did just that.

THE LAST PLACE I LOOKED

When I finally moved myself out of God's way, He was able to move in His mighty way. Only three months after making my vow to God, I finally agreed to meet the friend of a friend. He was a single guy named Scott. My friend, Molly, had been trying to get me to go out with him during my relationship hiatuses with Jeremy. I never agreed then, but now seemed like a good time.

On May 27, 2000, Molly and I picked up fried chicken from a fast food joint and set up a little picnic in Scott's front yard so we could meet. He was installing a sprinkler system in his backyard with two friends. After we assembled lunch, the three men came around the corner to greet us in the front yard. I remember thinking, "Oh, please let Scott be the guy in the yellow shirt. Oh, let him be the one in yellow."

I was thrilled when the handsome man in the yellow shirt extended his hand to shake mine and said, "Hi, I'm Scott."

Later in our relationship, he revealed to me that after our initial handshake, he walked around the corner and had his own interior dialogue. Apparently, his attraction echoed mine. He still describes the tan girl in the turquoise tank top and short jean overalls with a smile on his face. Our meeting was very casual as he was covered in mud from the sprinkler work. It was a sweet time. I found him to be kind, gentle, and handsome. I gave him my business card, granting him permission to call. Wasting no time, he called me the next day and asked me to dinner. I was thrilled he'd called and agreed to fit dinner in around my preparations to leave for camp as a counselor the following day.

He picked me up from my apartment and treated me to dinner at Macaroni Grill. We stumbled through getting to know one another, but it was lovely. After dinner, he offered to take me to the store to pick up some last minute items I needed for camp. He was thoughtful. We walked around the store looking for fun things to bring for my group of kids. When he brought me back to my apartment, I invited him to watch a movie. We had a great time laughing and talking, and when he left, he gave me a hug.

When I got home from camp, he called to ask about my week. We talked easily as the minutes passed. I told him my dad's company was hosting a family night at a Texas Rangers baseball game the following evening. They reserved an entire section, and I invited Scott to join us. It was a *free* Rangers game, who could pass that up? I made him aware that my parents, brother, uncle, and aunt would be there. He said he would love to go, but because of work and his volleyball game, he would meet me there instead of going together. He asked me to meet him for breakfast the next morning to give him his ticket. So, I met him at IHOP for a quick breakfast before he went to work. We left, excited to see each other that night.

My invitation to the game was not tied to any serious strings. I was going to be with my family, and I asked him to come along as a friend. I had just met him, after all, and I wasn't even sure if I was totally interested. Since my Bub and I lived together at this point, we rode to the game together. By the time the game started, Scott had not yet arrived. We did not have texting capabilities at that time, but I did carry a cell phone. He called me to let me know he was running late and would arrive soon. By this time I was very perturbed! I'm a punctual person and I find tardiness to be self-centered and rude. Anything kind I had thought of Scott before was quickly becoming muddied. With each passing inning, I compared him to every other jerk I dated in the past.

Near the middle of the game, my phone rang again. It was Scott. He said he had twisted his ankle during the volley-ball game. He thought it was best to stay off it and not come to the game. I know that conversation was not long because I wanted to hang up and never talk to him again. I hung up, turned to my brother, and said, "Yeah, he is a liar and an ass! He is just like every other guy on the planet!" I had zero tolerance after all I had been through over the years. My Bub's response was interesting and actually defensive of Scott, "You don't know that. He really could be telling the truth. You should give him a chance."

It didn't matter to me. I had never been stood up before, and this was as close as I wanted to get.

Later I found out he really did sprain his ankle playing volleyball. However, more truth would come to the surface. Evidently, when I said a lot of my family would be at the game, it freaked him out. He thought it was too early to meet family. He wasn't planning on not coming, but when he twisted his ankle, it gave him the perfect out.

I may or may not have been like a cat (and by cat, I mean lion) ready to pounce when he called me the next day. I was cleaning my apartment to let out some of my energy when the phone rang. I was cold as Scott rambled on about the previous night's mishap. At some point in the very brief conversation, he told me he didn't think it was the right time for us to start dating. I hung up and thought, "Right timing? It's not the right *lifetime* for you, dude!" I turned on the vacuum cleaner and went on my merry, single way. I'd like to say my response was completely healthy, but I may have had a little defense up. Or a big one. You see, I was serious about the vow I made to God. I had no interest in dating around. I was not going to waste my time on dead ends ever again.

MAKING ROOM

It turned out I would need those next few months to deal with more issues concerning my crazy ex-boyfriend, Jeremy. I wished he had gone away gracefully. But no. On the contrary. He decided if he couldn't have me, no one could. He did everything in his power to make my life miserable. He called me all the time. He left long, emotional messages on my voicemail. When he couldn't reach me via the phone, he followed me and even showed up at my work. He sent me flowers at work. He even showed up where I was babysitting, flashing the ring he was about to use to propose. I told him that a Godly (sober) man meant far more than the biggest diamond ring on earth. And I meant it.

I was forced to change my phone number several times because he would always track me down. It was exhausting. He talked his way back into my life so much in the past, he couldn't accept that he was unable to do so now. He kept pursuing to the point it became worrisome. In fact, I ended up filing a restraining order against him in two cities. My family and friends feared for my life. One morning, I forgot to set my alarm, and I didn't show up for work on time. All my co-workers and friends frantically called me and my family. They were convinced I had been hurt, or worse. We were all a little on edge. He was so unstable, we didn't put anything past him.

In the summer of 2000, I underwent knee surgery to repair damage from years of running track. I decided to stay at my parents' house so my mom could assist with my recovery. I was resting on a bed in the middle of my parents' den when my phone rang. I answered, surprised to hear Scott's voice on the other line. I had completely forgotten, but in the few short conversations we had in May, I mentioned when I was having surgery. He remembered the day, and called to ask me how it went. The conversation was brief and admittedly a little awkward. My mom entered the room as I hung up. I said, "You are never going to believe who just called me!"

My mom turned with a grin on her face and said, as if she was all-knowing, "Scott."

"How did you know?"

"I just figured he would call."

I must have been on heavy pain killers because I didn't give the situation much thought. I never questioned my mom as to why Scott was still lingering in her mind. Weeks passed as I recovered from surgery.

It was the end of July 2000. I walked into the apartment my Bub and I still shared after spending the weekend at my aunt's lake house. There was a note from my Bub on the kitchen counter. It read, "Scott Fullers or Fellers called." I immediately called Molly, the one who had introduced me to Scott almost two months earlier. I asked her what his last name was, because I had no clue. She answered, "Sellars. His name is Scott Sellars." Clearly, my Bub misheard the last name, and the Scott I met in May called me again. I debated whether I should call him back or not. I really hadn't thought of him. He didn't exactly leave me wanting more of him. But through the encouragement of a friend, I finally decided I would contact him. I waited nine days to finally return the phone call. I may have been a *little* stubborn. Nevertheless, when I called, it seemed like something was different. He sounded different to me. It sounded like he had spent the last two months working out whatever he needed to work out. I also had my fair share of junk to work through as I labored to totally free myself from old baggage. Scott's voice even sounded different. My interest was definitely heightened unlike when we first met. As we hung up, we both knew we would be talking again soon, although no plans were made.

CHIVALRY ISN'T DEAD

The last weekend in July I went out of town again. That Sunday, my phone rang as I was sitting out on the deck of my aunt's lake house. It was Scott, and he asked me out for that night! Typically, I would not suggest saying yes on such a short notice. However, something in me knew this would be something very different and that it was reasonable to accept. I told him I'd let him know when I arrived home. When I hung up the phone, I acted calm and collected. My mom and aunt, on the other hand, encouraged me to pack up immediately. They were super excited for me to go on a date with Scott. Determined to keep my chill, I packed up nonchalantly, said my goodbyes, and drove home (in record time).

Scott and I went to dinner and a movie. *The Patriot* is littered with some very emotional scenes. Of course I cried several times, but my embarrassment faded when I turned to see Scott tearing up as well. I thought, "Wow, what a tender, sweetheart of a guy."

Throughout the long movie, my post-surgery knee began to bother me. In the middle of the movie, I rubbed and fidgeted with my knee to deter the pain. He noticed my struggle and whispered, "If you need to stretch your leg out, you can rest it on my leg." He too had been through knee surgery so he empathized with me. I didn't see it as flirting, but as pure kindness. I'm sure it was a little of both, and of course I took him up on his offer. After a while, he rested his hand on my leg below my knee. I was shocked that such a simple gesture would send so many butterflies fluttering through my body. After the movie, as we were walking to the car, he took my hand in his. He drove me home and walked me upstairs to the front door of my apartment. We thanked each other for the great evening and hugged goodnight.

To say I was impressed with this guy was an understatement. No guy ever respected and treated me like such a precious gift! In my silly, nostalgic way, I floated over to my paper calendar, located the day's date, and wrote, "First Date with Scott" (with a few hearts beside it). Time froze as I noticed what day it was. I stared at my calendar in disbelief. It was July 29. My "un-wedding day," as I often referred to it. It was the day I was supposed to be married in 1995. Now, years later, God restored that date for me. I smiled, reflecting on the most wonderful date I just had with a man who would soon, and I mean *soon*, become my husband. It was a day that brought ill feelings for so long, but now it's one of my favorite days ever. I celebrate July 29 every year!

WHAT MATTERS

Isn't God amazing? He cares about the smallest, most intimate details of our lives! God is in the business of restor-
ing. He restores people. He restores situations. He can even
restore a bad memory, or in my case, a heartbreaking date
on my calendar.

Right when we least expect it, He will move on our behalf
and knock our socks off. We just need to get out of the way
and stop hindering the very thing we are desiring. For me, I
desired the man God had for me, but I kept dating people I
knew were not him.

FIND THE ROOT

Is there an area of your life that has not been fully submitted to God? Or is there something that needs to be surrendered? A thought pattern? A behavior? A relationship? Take time to really consider if you are personally causing any roadblocks to living the life God desires for you.

Do you have anything that needs to be restored in your life? God cares about the smallest of details. Be bold, have confidence, and begin praying and asking God for it, the Restorer of all things.

Chapter Six

I DO...I DO!

Scott was given many opportunities early in our relationship to show me, my family, and my friends just what a true gem he really is! Remember that crazy ex? Well, he still believed he could win me back. I remained friends with his brother and sister-in-law, so I think he was able to obtain some information about my life through them. They meant no harm, it just took them time to recognize the problem was more serious than they originally thought. They told him I was in a serious relationship, thinking it might encourage him to leave me alone for good.

Unfortunately, it backfired.

The same week Jeremy found out that I was dating someone, my tires were mysteriously slashed at my apartment *again*. As I walked out to my Explorer, I noticed it leaning to one side. I looked closer, and saw that two of my tires had been punctured. This was the second time in a year my car was the only car out of an entire parking lot that was "randomly" vandalized. My heart raced as I scanned the parking lot to see if I was being watched.

I ran upstairs and called Scott to relay the morning's events. At this point, most guys would have said, "Girl, you have too much baggage! I'm *gone!*" But not this guy. Not my Scott. He said what any dreamboat would, "Go into your apartment and wait for me. I am coming!"

He left work immediately and called for a tow truck. He scheduled and paid for my two tire replacements. If I hadn't already fallen in love with him, I would have in that instant! He came upstairs to comfort me. Scott became my defender and my hero that day. We all thought I would be safest if I moved back home with my parents. So that same night, Scott helped me move out of the apartment I shared with my Bub. By the next morning, I had a new address.

If ever there was a whirlwind romance, that is exactly what Scott and I had. He brought out a tender, gentle side of me that wasn't there before him. We complimented each other in every area. Where he was weak, I was strong, and vice versa. His pure, Godly love for me began to heal and silence Rejection's voice in my life. I felt Scott's love, and I felt God's love through Scott. I felt blessed to have a man that surpassed my lifelong dreams.

WHEN YOU KNOW, YOU KNOW

Within a month of dating, we knew we wanted to marry each other, although we hadn't yet spoken to one another about it. Scott and I went to a ranch with my family one weekend. I sat on a porch swing watching him play tennis with some of my family members. Just as the wind was blowing, I felt God blow something into my heart. He whispered, "That is your husband." I exhaled out of sheer relief as I thought, "Now this is supposed to be what it feels like." There was nothing forced. Nothing manipulated. It was just a peace that settled down deep in my soul. All my blood, sweat, and tears were worth it if, and only if, they led me to Scott. The Lord also spoke to Scott that day. Scott heard more of a, "How could you not marry her?" We came home excited for what the future would hold, but kept the Lord's words a secret from one another. We both were cautious and did not want to scare the other away from the relationship.

Once we confessed our intended future with one another, there was no need to take our time. We were two grown people with steady careers. A few months later, he proposed to me on November 21, 2000. We got married just over three months later on March 3, 2001. We met just nine months prior and only dated seven of those months. Our wedding was the most heavenly experience. It was peaceful. It was healing. It was perfect. We both cried through the whole ceremony. We were so thankful God had protected us from possible mistakes and saved us for each other! I joyfully removed my old engagement ring necklace. The future I hoped for had arrived in the form a tall, handsome darling. My promise to only marry who God intended was fulfilled. I gifted the necklace to a family member and made their day, because my day had been more than made.

The first six months of our marriage, we lived in a home he previously owned on a street named Jane Anne. Oh, the sweet times on Jane Anne were some of the happiest days of my life! I was finally a wife with a good husband. I laugh now, because it might have been offensive to him at the time, but I changed everything in that little house! It was a great house, but very much a bachelor pad. I painted walls, hung curtains, and brought in all new furniture. We did keep his dining room table though.

We entered our marriage excited about having children. I wanted four kids and he possibly wanted five. Because I was twenty-seven and he was thirty-two, we decided we shouldn't wait too long in case it took a while to conceive. After only five months of marriage, we decided to start trying. We were surprised when I got pregnant the very first month! We immediately decided to move into a better home in a better area.

AND THEN LIFE HAPPENS

I quit teaching the year we got married. I was so unhappy teaching in this particular school district that I quit and swore to never teach again. So I was pregnant and working at a little gift shop down the street. One day while I was at the shop, Scott called me, devastated. My head swirled as he told me he was just laid off from his corporate job. He was employed by American Airlines for sixteen years. Because 9/11 greatly affected the travel industry, his company decided to downsize. They chose to let Scott go due to his seniority and pay. Talk about a gut punch! We found ourselves in a new house, pregnant with our first baby, and jobless. Our happily ever-after was becoming tainted by harsh reality.

Scott quickly found another job in the same industry. It was perfect timing, right before I delivered Elijah Scott in May 2002. Unfortunately, the aftermath of 9/11 didn't cease altering the travel industry. In October 2003, I had just given birth to our second son, Ean Samuel. Scott returned to work after his paternity leave. That morning, everyone in the office threw him a baby shower. That afternoon, his boss handed him an empty box and told him to gather his things. We would survive the next nine months with no job and very little hope. Being stuck at home with a newborn and a child under two years old was intense. The stress quickly mounted.

Scott once again gained employment in the same industry just in time for me to take another positive pregnancy test. I will never know if it was the stress, but I ended up losing our baby. It was such a sad and humbling time. I had coined the nickname "Fertile-Myrtle" since the wind would blow and I would become pregnant. I felt like a super woman! I had two great pregnancies and births. I never considered the possibility of miscarriage. As my nickname would prove true, against the doctor's best advice, I got pregnant again the following month. I gave birth to my sweet girl, Ella Kate, in September 2005. Scott's job was going well at this time. Things seemed to be solid for a few years. Miraculously, we always had insurance each time I gave birth. It was no different when I had our fourth and final baby, Ezra Joseph, in February 2007.

Scott wanted five children and I wanted four; it turns out we both got our way. One baby in heaven, four babies on earth.

Only six years into our marriage, we found ourselves with four children under five. It was crazy. It really was. Most of our days were spent merely surviving. We had lots of playdates and stayed very busy. If I had to do it all over again though, I wouldn't change a thing! Our home was full of giggles, diapers, toys, hugs, tears, kisses, energy, and fun. We were surrounded by four perfect, healthy babies. I felt blessed to be a stay-at-home mom and raise my own kids.

Our fourth child was not even one year old yet when, to our shock, Scott got laid off for the third time in our short six years of marriage. This resulted in very dark days and scary times. Scott decided it was best to steer clear of the corporate world, at least in the field of his expertise. He worked years doing whatever he could to keep a roof over our heads and food on the table. The Lord worked supernaturally during this time. We never lost our house, cars, or anything else. It wasn't always what we wanted, but we ate. We learned true dependence on God like never before. Our church and friends stepped in a few times to cover our lack. That season birthed a faith in both Scott and I that forever changed us. Scott finally settled into something that brought him both joy and opportunity. He landed on general contracting and storm restoration of houses and commercial properties. He found his niche. He sailed.

THAT OLD, UNWANTED FRIEND

Rejection had been silenced for a while at this point, in large part thanks to Scott's love and provision. After all, I was living my dreams with the love of my life! I knew I had a forever spouse, which brought great peace. Even when everything else seemed hopeless, I felt very solid with my husband, and that made all the difference. Inside my marriage, Rejection lost some power, so it got creative and began attacking me from the outside. In turn, it greatly affected my marriage. In the first years of our marriage we went through some painful experiences involving other people we love.

We had one set of couple friends who, to my surprise, revealed they didn't like me for Scott. In fact, in a roundabout way, Scott's friend told him he married the wrong person! I received a lengthy, typed letter in the mail that listed all my flaws, slicing me to the core. The letter explained in detail how I was failing in every area of my life. They were "trying to help me be a better person and wife." They went so far as to say I was a terrible daughter-in-law, a role I took great pride in because I adored my new parents. I was beyond devastated. In all my life, I never received scrutiny so cruel. Rejection barged into my life again—not like a powerful wind, but a level five hurricane.

Scott and I agreed it was all ludicrous and just an attack from the enemy. The only problem was Scott and I disagreed about how to handle it. Scott was passive and non-confrontational. He thought it was nonsense and that we should ignore it. He thought we needed to move on and away from such toxicity. He didn't think it deserved any attention. On the contrary, I was not passive and believed in grabbing the bull by the horns. To a woman who struggled with Rejection and believed in justice, ignoring it was the worst idea! This was our first major fight of many. We settled in a constant state of disagreement over this issue. It was sadly the first time we raised our voices toward one another in very "heated fellowships." All I wanted was for my knight in shining armor, who had protected me so many times before, to defend what was righteous. Because Scott wasn't defending me and our marriage, I felt that he was rejecting me.

Scott eventually grew tired of my pleading (or of our fighting) and called his friend. My husband rose up and defended what I felt the Lord wanted defended. God held this as a high priority since He stated in Mark 10:9, "Therefore, what God joined together, let no one separate." I was infuriated that anyone would try to come between our God-given marriage! I was listening in as he reprimanded him, "How dare you say anything about my marriage!" Scott passionately scolded him and told him where to shove it. That settled it. That was all I needed. It also helped that many close friends and relatives affirmed me in all the areas in which I had been obliterated. I was then able to lick my wounds, count my losses, and move on. I just wanted a righteous anger to rise in Scott, and when it did, all was well.

A few years later we weathered a similar situation, except with family members. I was distressed when I sensed some serious animosity toward me from a member of Scott's family. I questioned one of Scott's parents about this person's behavior. They revealed everything to me, and I was sorry I asked. They told me about a slew of things that was said behind my back, dating all the way to the beginning of our marriage. I was totally wrecked. This family member was offended even with some of my wedding decisions. Rejection roared like a tsunami, hurling accusations and judgments.

For a season I did not want to attend functions with Scott's family. I felt like I was under a microscope. Every move or statement I made was being watched and judged incorrectly and unfairly. I couldn't do anything right. Kicking and screaming, I was dragged to family events, and I cried all the way home. A day after a family gathering, I would often receive hurtful feedback. Something I said or did was twisted in a way that defiled my character. Being aware of what was being said behind my back, I sensed the rejection seeping in the second I walked into the room. I felt Rejection waiting to greet me at these gatherings. I felt unloved and unwanted. It was not the family I thought I married into years ago, the family I loved and thought loved me.

As the enemy would have it, this caused major problems in our marriage. It caused even more problems than our friend conflict, because this was family. Once again, Scott and I were in a constant state of disagreement concerning this matter. I wanted Scott to defend the false accusations and wrong judgments. Due to the season this particular family member was in, Scott thought it would fall on deaf ears. Although he was shocked at their behavior, he thought it wasn't worth the effort because hurt people hurt people. Scott thought if 99% of the people in our lives felt one way, then we should not focus on the 1% who felt the opposite way. Again, Rejection was right in my face, eager to remind me that my husband wasn't defending me and therefore, rejecting me. Rejection *did* cloud my marriage. It found a new way into my heart.

Sadly, the family situation continued for years. It caused more problems in my marriage than anything ever had because it didn't stop. A part of me thought if Scott wasn't defending me, perhaps he agreed with this person. Scott felt torn because it was his family, and family was harder to navigate. He did begin to pull away from some of his family as he lost more and more respect for them. There was a shift when he began to cleave to me and leave family problems behind. Everything came to an all-time low when I was accused of stealing. The absurdity of this accusation heated Scott to his boiling point. He confronted the situation fearlessly and demanded an apology. He declared we would not attend any more family functions until there was restitution. I received, via Scott's conversation, an "I am sorry if she was offended," and that was it. We both decided we had to move on. Scott defended me, so the damage done to our marriage began to heal. Sure, it would be nice to be liked by *all* his family, but I finally accepted it may not be possible. My focus was my marriage. As long as there was peace and unity in my marriage, I could deal with anything that came my way, even being disliked by someone we loved.

Eventually, things settled down in Scott's family. His family members were going through their own share of heartache. Their attention finally turned away from me. Family functions became a rarer occurrence over the years. They were much more bearable when I didn't feel torn apart. Now, after seventeen years of being in the family, we all seem to enjoy one another when we are together. The past is water under the bridge. We have all grown to appreciate one another. We all have choices to make in the face of disunity, slander, and distrust. We chose to stand firm in love, and that changed the entire course.

WHAT MATTERS

When we are robbed of our security, in any area of life, we are shaken. Life becomes unstable. The future becomes unclear. It can leave us feeling insecure, scared, and even hopeless. Life as we know it can change in an instant with a job loss, a death, or in my case, other people wrongfully judging me.

Too bad we tend to care so much about what other people think, right? This can consume our thoughts and lives when we deeply desire justice and truth to be defended. When waves of disappointment crash all around us, our happily ever after can seem happily ever never! Consider which relationships in your life are most important, and nourish, guard, and defend those. And when other relationships bring disappointment, focus in gratitude on the ones you've built on a firm foundation.

FIND THE ROOT

Dear friend, if you are single, I know you may be waiting for your own happily ever after. I pray you find peace and contentment in your singleness first. I pray you won't settle as you patiently wait on God's best.

Is there someone who has wrongfully judged your character, causing you deep pain? I am fully convinced acceptance is the cure for Rejection. Surround yourself with people who affirm you and do not tear you down, people who look for the good in you and not the bad, and people who overlook your few flaws because of your plethora of redeeming qualities! Most importantly, receiving God's acceptance will make you fully confident in *who* you are and *Whose* you are. Then, the darts of the enemy lose their power.

Chapter Seven

AN APPOINTED TIME

We started attending a new church in 2004. My immediate sense was that there was something different about this church than ones I attended in the past. The pastor was gifted and anointed to preach God's Word from the Bible in ways I had never witnessed. The Word became alive and real to me. Scripture I read my whole life took on new meaning. My eyes were opened anew, seeing God and the Holy Spirit in new, glorious light. It was like the time I turned forty and didn't know I couldn't see well anymore until I put on someone else's readers and saw everything clearly. The things of God came into perspective. I grew hungry to learn more about God and discover what He had for my life. If there was more of God, I wanted it!

NO MORE RUNNING

Through the grapevine, I learned that the Freedom Department in my church offered a two-day event called *Kairos*. *Kairos* is a Greek word that means "opportune time." It was time set aside to listen to teachings, hear from God, and clean out the junk in your life. I could not grasp the fact that there was an entire department dedicated to *freedom*. The word itself was a new concept for me. This church wanted every person to hear from God about who He is and about who we were in Him. They were dedicated to helping people get free of junk in their lives and hearts. They offered people tools to live life victoriously. I attended my first *Kairos* in 2008. It was strategically designed and broken up into sections.

The first section established identity and walked us through how to hear from God. It focused on grace and receiving God's forgiveness. The leaders explained that a stronghold was a wrong pattern of thought about ourselves, others, or situations. They gave us time to assess our own thoughts and provided tools to help alter any destructive thinking.

The second section focused on cleaning up our hearts by getting rid of generational iniquities, unhealthy heart attachments, and shame.

The third section went into depth about healing. Forgiveness was key to healing our own hearts. This was when they talked about *Rejection* and father/mother wounds.

As I lived through those two days, I searched deeply in my soul. I was shocked to realize how much junk from my past relationships continued to rear its ugly head in my present ones. Even though Scott was nothing like the other guys I dated, deep down I remained afraid he would turn out to be like them. If he showed the slightest hint of any grouchy behavior, I immediately labeled him a jerk. Without realizing it, I was comparing him and holding him accountable for past people's offenses. It definitely didn't produce good fruit to sustain a healthy marriage.

During this weekend, I specifically faced Rejection head-to-head. In almost every relationship in my life, I couldn't escape feelings of rejection. Just like weeding your garden, true healing comes when you dig out the root. In prayer, I asked God to reveal a time when I first felt rejected. Immediately, a memory popped into my head of an incident in the fifth grade when I was made to feel poor and inferior. I closed my eyes, pushed through the pain, and allowed myself to remember.

It was the year they were testing out open concept classrooms, so the classrooms in my school were only separated by some cubbies and shelves (thankfully they ditched that idea—it was too noisy). I was sitting in my desk toward the back of the room before school officially started for the day. I felt exceptionally proud that morning. The previous weekend, only a handful of fifth graders were invited to a sixth grade party. I was one of the chosen ones. It was my first time to play spin-the-bottle. In the '80s, it only required a peck on the cheek or a super quick kiss on the lips. The bottle landed on me once. So my cheek had been kissed by one of the popular older guys. Naturally, my head was in the clouds.

A few mornings later, a friend of mine pointed toward two cubbies and said, "They want to talk to you." As I looked over, I saw them. I thought, "Wait, they want to talk to me?" They were only the most popular boys in the sixth grade. And they were waiting for me by the bookcase, looking so fine! I nervously, yet proudly, walked over to them. I greeted them awkwardly, smiling through my nerves.

They asked a perplexing question, "Did you have fun last night?"

I paused and quickly replayed the weekend in my head, "Uh, last night?" I thought they were possibly trying to refer to my kiss on Friday night.

They laughed, mocking me, "Yeah, at K-Mart! We called you last night and your Dad said you weren't home because you went to K-Mart!"

I would have preferred to be buried alive. They knew. I went to K-Mart with my mom the night before. My sweet dad, unaware that his honesty would destroy my reputation, told those boys I was not home because I went to K-Mart with my mom. Just like that, the cat was out of the bag: I shopped at K-Mart.

You see, to snotty Arlington kids who thought they were rich, K-Mart was a place only poor people shopped. It was the store kids used in hurling insults at someone. If someone wanted to make fun of your shirt, they would say, "Where did you get that? K-Mart?" It was always followed by jeers and snickers. It may sound like the most ridiculous thing, but this knowledge of my family's shopping expedition gave them the power to label me poor and low class.

I had floated out of my chair to meet them, yet I found myself crawling, humiliated, back to my seat.

At this event, I prayed and asked God to remove the feelings of shame attached with that memory and to heal my heart. I believe He did. I know He resurfaced that memory for a reason. The Lord made so much progress on my heart that weekend, but I left *Kairos* feeling like something was still wrong with me. I questioned God, "How can I be free of this thing if I can't figure out exactly what it is or where it came from?"

That weekend was the beginning of the freedom train chugging in my life. It revealed a lot, but more was to come.

JUST JEALOUSY?

As a grown, married woman, I did not like the mess that kept appearing in my heart and in my life. I had a lot of really good friends. The Lord blessed Scott and I with some lifelong best friends. We were surrounded by Godly relationships. However, I struggled with Rejection on a weekly basis.

Like I mentioned before, when I felt like Scott did not defend me or our marriage, I felt as though he was rejecting me personally. As a result, I built walls around my heart to insulate and protect myself. We experienced seasons in our marriage where there would be a distance the size of the Grand Canyon between us. We were sitting next to each other on the couch, but we might as well have been on different planets. When my need for Scott's love and acceptance was not adequately met, I would search for it through friendships. When my priorities were out of order, it added insult to injury. I placed too much emphasis on my friendships. They became my focus, and I expected them to fulfill a need friendships weren't designed to fill.

So it was in my friendships that Rejection wielded the most power. The most unattractive jealousy would seep to the surface of my heart. If one friend would go out with another friend, I would run an internal dialogue:

"She wanted to go out with her and not me."

"She must like her more than me."

"I must not be as fun as her."

I couldn't even bring myself to ask them if they had a good time when they went out together. If a friend told me about how much fun she had, I would change the subject. It was painful to hear. As these thoughts danced in my mind, I grew frustrated with myself. I was relieved none of my friends knew what I was thinking or feeling. If they knew, I was certain they would no longer want to be my friend.

Social media posts were just about the death of me! Facebook taunted me every Monday morning. Before there was Facebook, if someone had a great weekend without me, I was never aware. Out of sight, out of mind. Bliss. The internet age took my brokenness to a new level. My inner turmoil was validated in the form of tiny pixels. Everyone was having a blast and it didn't matter that I wasn't there. I did not fit in. I felt uninvited because I was uninvited. I felt unwanted because social media displayed all the girls who did not want me at their birthday dinners. Forget about me liking the post or even wishing them a happy birthday! Then they would know I saw the picture. And I didn't want them to know I saw it. What if they knew I was hurt? I refused to let others know how I was feeling. It was unattractive, and I knew it.

Social media also offered me a front row seat to the many girls' nights I missed. I was able to see where they ate and even what they ate! Food postings were my nemesis. I scrolled through the photos of the cute dresses and high-heeled shoes they wore, while I sat at home in my pajamas. I had concrete evidence that everyone was having loads of fun while we were stuck at home most weekends with no plans and no invitations.

Thanks to the internet, I was able to see all the couples who did not want Scott and me on their couples date, or better yet, their vacations. They posted about where they ate, what they ate, and what movie they saw. Like a glutton for punishment, I would sit at my computer and scroll and scroll. I would scroll and feel sick. I would scroll and feel unwanted. I would scroll and feel unloved. It was driving me nuts!

So I would stop scrolling and talk to my own brain. "You are a Godly, *grown* woman. Quit it! For crying out loud, you are a wife and mom, grow up! You have lots of friends! You *do* have a social life. You are a leader in church. You can't let people see this immaturity!"

I led a ladies group in my home with great success. My parenting wisdom actually changed some new moms' lives. I led small groups of ladies at church. I possessed plenty of knowledge. I was making an impact in women's lives all the time. I just had a brokenness that lurked right below the surface of who I was. Most frustratingly, I didn't know how to fix it.

Leaders are held to such a higher standard. And to a certain degree, they should be. But their human side, their fallen, vulnerable side is often overlooked or dismissed. Often leaders are incorrectly judged as being perfect people who have it all together. All leaders, even the ones you hold highest on your pedestal, are just people with imperfect lives who need a Savior. I knew I needed my Savior to eradicate my fleshy garbage.

I did my best to muster up feelings of the fruit of the Spirit like love, joy, and peace. I would try to *act* better, but I had a high fail rate! I knew I didn't want to be this way. I was sprinting in a hamster wheel of feeling rejected and trying hard to *not* feel rejected!

It wasn't until the following year that truth began to reveal itself in my life, and I finally received answers to life-long questions. God was about to unearth roots I never knew existed. He was about to shine His light on truth that would heal me and set me free. So free that I rarely deal with this particular jealousy in my life anymore.

WHAT MATTERS

This must be why Paul says in Romans 7:15, "For what I want to do I do not do, but what I hate I do." We have all acted in ways we wish we hadn't. We say things we know we shouldn't. All of us all have desires to improve various areas of our life. Sometimes we just get stuck and we need help getting unstuck!

Let's just be real about social media. The images people are putting out for everyone to see are the best version of themselves, while the enemy is pointing out the *worst* version of you! It's also good to remember most pictures we see have been altered or filtered. I know I'm guilty of this practice. It's just too tempting to remove a wrinkle here and there! There are people whose house is a wreck, but post pictures at the correct angle to make it appear like it belongs in a magazine. There are people whose marriages are crumbling, but on Facebook they appear like they're living in a constant honeymoon phase. Most people post what they want people to believe about them, but may not be the full truth.

FIND THE ROOT

Have you ever struggled with Rejection? How have the enemy's lies or deception led you to a place of rejection or feelings of inadequacy? Ask God to reveal where this began. Ask God to show you the lies you are believing. Ask Him to heal you of the root cause.

Do you deal with insecurities in relationships, especially friendships? Pray and ask God to reveal what is causing this. The more time you spend with God and find security in who He has created you to be, the less you will feel insecure.

Social media has a lot of positives. But it can sometimes do more damage than good. How much time are you devoting to a social media world versus your real life right in front of you? Maybe limit your daily screen time. Maybe put it down entirely for a season. Ask God if He wants to speak to you in this area.

Chapter Eight

TIME HEALS NOTHING

———————

The year 2009 was a year marked with unbelievable tragedy and loss in my story. One warm evening in June, I received a phone call that would change my life forever. My Aunt Lyanna was on the other end, speaking words that would crush my heart in an instant, "Dana, Eric was found face down on his kitchen floor and they are rushing him to the hospital. It doesn't look good. You need to come."

In desperation for air, I ran outside to my driveway. Panic engulfed me. "What do you mean? What is it?"

"He was already blue. They think drugs were involved."

I don't remember the remainder of that conversation because my only focus was getting to the hospital.

I would have been a danger to society had I driven myself, so my husband offered to drive me. My four children were asleep and a friend came over to watch them. The twenty-minute drive to the hospital felt like an hour! I am certain I scared my husband, because I scared myself! In my fear, I was coming out of my skin and almost out of my seatbelt. I was hoping and believing for the best, but something deep within me knew otherwise.

NOT OLD ENOUGH TO HANDLE THIS

I flew into the emergency room and asked to see Eric Wagnon. It was almost like they expected me. They pointed through the doors and said, "Down the hall on the left."

What? He was in a room?

I ran down the long hallway and caught sight of the room. Hope rose within me. He was in a room, he was stable. But as my view of the room became clearer, my heart stopped. I saw an empty bed. I scanned the room and saw other family members standing, waiting. My parents were sitting in some chairs next to the empty bed. My sister was there. My aunt was standing there, too.

I frantically asked, "Where is he?"

Numb with desperation, they replied, "We don't know, they haven't told us anything yet."

Flashes of every ER-themed television show I watched over the years overwhelmed my mind. As panic spread through my veins like liquid fire I shouted, "This is not good! They brought us back here to tell us something. They called us to a private room for a reason!"

More people filled the room. My parents' pastor and his wife arrived. My sister's mother was waiting in the hall. Then I turned and saw her, Amy, my brother's girlfriend of three years. She is the one who found him face down on the kitchen floor in the apartment they shared. She walked in, guided by her older sister. It was obvious she was either still high or coming off of some serious drugs. She looked like a user. Both sisters were known to have drug addictions for years. We, however, were under the assumption she was now clean, although we hadn't seen her in almost a year. One look at her and we realized she was not clean. The sisters cowardly walked in with heads down and stood against the wall.

I was so angry with the sight before my eyes, but the Holy Spirit whispered gently, "Hug her."

Wait. What?

I, Dana, in my flesh, wanted to attack her! I did not want to see her nor did I think she belonged in the room with our family. She was not family. Not even close.

Two days before this, on Father's Day, my Bub told us he was finally leaving Amy that week because of their toxic relationship. He had a friend coming to help him move on Wednesday. It was Tuesday night. We were ready for him to wash his hands of her. But there she was, in the room, and I felt like God wanted me to hug her. In a moment of sheer grace, I thought about what it must feel like to be in her shoes. As I took a few steps toward her. Her physical stature hinted that a hug was the last thing she expected from me. I wrapped my arms around her for a moment, then returned to sitting on the end of the bed.

I tried to make eye contact with her and asked, "Amy, what was it? What did he take? What drug was it?"

Her answer was deplorable. She said in a sheepish but certain voice, "Cocaine."

I gasped and cried out. You see, through the years of my brother's addiction, his weakness was never drugs; it was always alcohol. In his early years, he told me about drugs he tried, but his first choice was alcohol. *Always.* Now, he was thirty-eight years old, and according to what we knew, drugs weren't an issue for almost twenty years.

The doctor finally entered the room. He started calmly, "When we brought Eric in…"

Before he could finish, my mom interrupted, her voice cracking in hysteria, "Is my son alive or dead?"

His answer altered our family forever, "I'm so sorry."

Wait. Stop. Do not finish that sentence!

"We did everything we could, but he did not make it."

He did not make it? HE DID NOT MAKE IT!

The sounds that erupted in that room haunt me to this day. It was the sound of unfathomable, heart-wrenching devastation. My parents exploded in complete grief. I began to moan and cry. My sister fell down between the bed and the wall in a near panic attack. My aunt, through her own tears, was trying to get my sister to stand and breathe. My parents' pastor was trying to get us to calm down. We all struggled to breathe as our hearts suffocated in agony.

Not long after, we were ushered out of that awful room and led into an even more horrific room: the one where Eric's body laid. It was so surreal. There was my sweet Bub, resting on the metal table with a sheet pulled up to his chest. Not alive. Dead. Honestly, he just looked asleep. I wanted to yell, "Get up. Wake up, Bub!"

My sister walked into the room and immediately noticed dried blood in his nose. It was probably caused by him falling face first on the kitchen floor. She found it suspicious that my brother died the night before he was going to leave Amy. She thought there might have been foul play; I actually entertained the thought as well. We all agreed two addicts were toxic to one another. But there was only one certain reality that screamed in our face: our Bub overdosed. He was the one who was gone.

We will never know what happened that night. I am not sure I want to know. I thought of my Bub one way, and I'd like to keep those thoughts on the forefront of my mind. Clearly he was living a dark life filled with secrets he kept from everyone, except Amy. His co-workers, including his best friend, were in disbelief. They had no idea he used drugs either. His addiction robbed him of an abundant life and ultimately robbed him of his very life. I never anticipated a drug overdose. I would not have been shocked by alcohol poisoning or a jail sentence due to vehicular manslaughter. But this? This blindsided us.

I darted outside the hospital and called my best friend who was watching my kids. I really don't remember a thing I said. I am certain I was a rambling, hysterical mess. I had a somber moment when I realized I was going to have to tell my four sweet kids, who adored their Uncle Bub, that he was gone forever. I hung up and confessed to my mom's friend, "I am not old enough to handle this!"

In that moment, I didn't feel like a wife and mom. I felt like a little sister who just needed her big brother.

Telling my kids turned out to be worse than I imagined. At the time, they were seven, six, four, and two years old. Scott and I called Eli and Ean, the two oldest, into the living room first. They sat on our ottoman, and we sat across from them on the couch. I carefully delivered the horrible news in the gentlest way I could, as I was still processing the new reality myself. I prepared myself for sadness and tears. But honestly, I wasn't sure they were even old enough to understand the gravity and finality of death. Boy, was I wrong! Eli, the oldest, threw himself across the couch and began to wail into the pillow. He moaned, "No. No! He's *dead*?!"

Taking a cue from his big brother, Ean came to understand and sobbed hysterically. We fell like dominoes. Scott and I wept as we extended comfort to our little ones. I was bearing the heartache of all four of my kids, while simultaneously maneuvering through my own grief. I thought I might cease existing, right there on my living room sofa. Ella saw her two brothers crying and made her way down the path of hysteria. Poor Ezra walked in the room to find his five family members wailing, moaning, and crying. Having no clue what was going on, he immediately burst into tears. The six of us huddled together, hugging and sobbing. It was the hardest parenting moment of my life.

BROKEN HEART SYNDROME

The next several days involved non-stop funeral plans, arrangements, and visitors. I stayed at my parents' house for several days. I couldn't bring myself to leave them. For this season, I had nothing to give as a wife and mom. I struggled to function in those roles. I could only function in my role as a daughter and sister. I wanted to be in my parents' home as much as possible. My friends knew it and filled in where I was weak. Three of my friends, Marci, Maria, and Jenn, became my "Three Musketeers." They swooped in and worked together beautifully. They took over my calendar and my kids and kept our home fires burning.

A few weeks after my Bub's death, my mom's health began to decline. She began acting really weird, and we couldn't put our finger on the reason. One evening, we noticed she looked awfully pale. My dad decided to take her to a clinic near their house. The room closed in on them when the doctor came in and said, "Her EKG is showing that she had a heart attack.

We are going to have to send her downtown for further testing." She was transferred by ambulance to a nearby hospital. I could not believe my ears when my dad called to tell me. I rushed to the hospital in a panic.

I walked in and heard her saying, "I just buried my son last week. I just buried my son."

We were all thinking the same thing.

Intrigued by her unique scenario, the doctor on-call wanted to know more about what was going on with my mom. The doctors began to suspect my mom may not have suffered a heart attack like they initially thought. The doctor ordered more tests to search for better answers. One test revealed my mom suffered stress cardiomyopathy, or "broken heart syndrome." Excessive stress resulting from traumatic events can stun or shock the heart, giving the impression of a heart attack. The stress of losing my brother was too much for my mom to bear. By the grace of God, these further tests revealed something crucial. My mom's left artery was 80% closed. She was a heart attack waiting to happen. My mom needed double by-pass heart surgery. Further, the medical professionals believed she was too high risk and that no doctor would want to touch her. They gave up without a fight, "If she could find someone to do her surgery, she probably wouldn't make it through due to her fragile state."

Panic.

Fear.

Grief.

We all felt overwhelmed. This was too much. My dad and husband each grabbed one of my arms to keep me from falling to the floor. I couldn't lose my brother and my mom. I wouldn't survive it.

Thankfully, what the test consultant didn't know was that my God had a different plan. The number one heart surgeon at the number one heart hospital in the area was confident he could he could repair my mom's heart. And that is just what he did. Two weeks after my Bub died, my mom underwent double bi-pass heart surgery. I know. It was crazy then, and it's even crazier to look back and remember that horrible time. Only the Lord made it possible to endure two emotionally traumatic events only weeks apart. God breathed through us on the days we struggled to breathe on our own.

A confusing scenario developed after our tragic loss, however. Because of my mom's health issues, all our grief was put on a shelf. The family did not have time to properly grieve my Bub because our emotions, energy, and attention were all focused on one thing: Mom *had* to get better. We could not lose another immediate family member. She was on the forefront of our hearts and minds.

By God's grace, my mom regained her health. Her heart was repaired, at least physically. A year passed before my grief really hit me. And it came like a freight train. My life revolved around four children, and my alone time was very limited. So my grief would consume me when I was alone in the car between school drop-offs, practices, and errands. I shouted at my Bub, or God, or just sobbed uncontrollably. When I concentrated on the finality of his death, anxiety washed over me like a monsoon. *Every single time.* The thought that for the rest of my life on earth, I would never ever see, hug, hear, or talk to my Bub again was enough to crush me. Even today, years later, pondering this fact still consumes me in a matter of seconds. My only comfort is knowing I will see him in heaven, because he had a relationship with Jesus.

Swallowed by her own grief, my sister pulled away from the rest of us. She filled her time with her job, leaving little time for the family. With both siblings seemingly absent from my life, I felt like I was no longer a sister. This became one of the heaviest burdens I carried. I cried out to God one day in my car, "How do I go from being a sister to not being a sister?"

I didn't know how to not be a sister. It was a part of my identity.

As my heart routinely broke and I ached to be a sister, I revisited my lifelong questions. A specific part of my mom's story of my conception lingered in my mind. Remember when she told John she was pregnant with me? She learned that his wife was pregnant as well. I couldn't shake the curiosity about this intriguing possibility: If John was my biological father, it meant the daughter he had with his wife would be my sister. I didn't know how or when, but I finally acknowledged that these questions would one day need to be answered. I wouldn't be at peace otherwise.

WHAT MATTERS

Losing someone is one of life's most painful events. Losing someone tragically is even worse. It's so sudden. It's so final. There is no warning. It can show up and rob you of your own life.

It leaves you wondering if your last conversation was a good one. Did you tell them you loved them enough? God says he knows the number of days we have on this earth, but we do not share that privilege. We should live as if we are not promised another day and treat those in our lives the same way.

FIND THE ROOT

Most of us have experienced our own degree of "broken heart syndrome." Our hearts get broken all the time. We lose loved ones or friends. We lose jobs and people break promises. We have moments when things turn out different than we imagined. Holding hands with Grief is hard and lonely. Don't we wish the rest of the world would just stop so we can catch our breath? Time doesn't stop. You just learn to live life differently as the waves of remembrance and grief ebb and flow. Go with the flow. Grieve however you need to grieve.

Can you reflect on a time when you received bad news, or you were in the midst of a situation that looked bleak? Did you have a "but God" moment? When did God shed light? When did He turn it around? Take time to remember the faithfulness of God in that moment.

Do you or anyone you know struggle with addiction? It's not the absence of *something* that frees one from addiction, it is the *presence* of Someone! God has the power to totally eradicate addiction. In addition to God's working power, there are great facilities that guide addicts on a path of sobriety and healing. Teen Challenge (regardless of the name, it's for all ages) takes a holistic treatment approach. Go to teenchallengeusa.com to find locations near you for yourself or a loved one.

Chapter Nine

DIGGING FOR THE ROOT

It was the summer of 2011. I wasn't completely consumed with thoughts and questions, but the truth about my conception was on my mind daily. I wanted to know if John was my biological father, but I didn't know how to find out. My main concern when considering this search was my daddy. Unless my mom told him, he was never aware of my questioning. I did not want to hurt him. More importantly, I didn't want him to think I wanted a different father. Even though I wondered over the years, I never needed or wanted to know until now. I didn't have a gaping father wound that left me wishing for a different dad. I loved my daddy and didn't need another one. But what if I had more siblings? In the wake of my losses, who couldn't use a few more siblings, right?

DETECTIVE DANA

At this time, I wasn't ready to discuss this with my parents. They were clueless about my recent wrestling with these thoughts and feelings. My parents were still so deep in their own grief over my brother, I definitely didn't want to add to their pain. So I began my search with my dad's sister. My "Nantie," as I call her, was the next best thing to my parents. She was a teenager at the time I was conceived. She lived with my mom before and after my birth. I knew she would have firsthand memories about the events surrounding my birth. In hindsight, I see that God sent me to her house that day because what I learned about my past from her was crucial to my present. Certain situations weren't hidden from me maliciously but were omitted from the narrative in order to protect me. Being with my aunt gave me the freedom to ask some burning questions that I would never have asked my mom.

As I sat on my aunt's couch, I fired the questions one after another. I'm sure she wondered why, at thirty-nine years old, I suddenly felt compelled to interrogate her about events from 1972. I wasn't after a specific answer, but I wanted to learn about her memories. I asked her to tell me anything and everything she remembered from before I was conceived, to when my Mom was pregnant, to after I was born. We talked for hours. Then, a tidal wave of revelation appeared.

A question flew out of my mouth before I had time to even consider the implications of its answer. In turn, my aunt revealed something I never knew.

"Did anyone want my mom to abort me?"

She admitted that, because of the situation, my mom was in at the time, it was suggested that her pregnancy be terminated. In fact, my mom's doctor was the first one to suggest it. He offered, "I can help take care of this, you know," as if I were a problem my mom could toss away like an outdated handbag. My aunt painfully revealed that my very own grandmother hinted to such a "solution". She believed my mom's life was such a mess that she definitely didn't need to bring another baby into it.

My aunt continued to share, oblivious to the avalanche demolishing my soul. I dwelled on the fact that I was verbally rejected before I was even born. But, glory to God, my mother never considered abortion to be an option. She held a strong conviction regarding the subject. Plus, I think she hoped another baby would help bring her and my dad together for good.

During my visit with my aunt, I also discovered details about the first few hours after my birth. Apparently, family members shuffled into the hospital with the sole intention of getting a good look at me. More specifically, to get a good look at my looks. My dad's family wanted to see if I looked like Freddie or John. Since both families knew my mom had been with both men, some questioned which one was really my father. They even placed bets. Honestly, this troubled my heart more than the suggestion of abortion. My precious first hours of life were filled with questioning and ridicule instead of acceptance and celebration. Not only was my value tossed aside while in the womb, it was now demeaned to an entertaining guessing game.

I returned home from my aunt's house an emotional wreck. I collapsed in a kitchen chair and my head dropped onto the smooth wood of the table. My husband heard me trying to muffle the sound of my crying. These were the first tears I ever shed over this subject.

As I cried, I confessed to Scott, "I think I'm bothered! I think I'm bothered by all of this. Before, I didn't need to know, but now I feel like I must know! I may have another sibling. I just want answers. I just want the truth!"

I shared with him some previously undisclosed details my aunt shared with me and how it made me feel. My husband began pacing the floor.

"What do you want? We can do a DNA test between you and your sister. Maybe we can get a sample off her drinking glass! If you don't share DNA with her, then it means you don't share DNA with your dad!"

I stopped him from jumping off the cliff. I explained I needed to first pray hard and seek God's wisdom.

The next day, my friend Marci was over at my house. I filled her in on what I learned from my aunt and how I was feeling as a result. Her reaction was instant and certain, "There's your root of rejection! It was spoken over you in the womb!" I was so overwhelmed and emotional the day before, I never stopped to process the importance of the information I digested. But now, in the middle of my sunroom, my cloudy eyes were cleared. I could see the root of rejection! We embraced and cried. Marci knew me well. She knew I longed for this particular healing.

Providentially, I was already signed up to attend another Kairos the following week. During the session on rejection, I prayed for God to remove the root and heal my heart of it for good. As I prayed, I had a vision of a large hand grasping the trunk of a tree. The tree was ripped out of the ground with a lot of gnarly roots attached. The Holy Spirit showed me that it was a root of Rejection from my conception, and it was being healed. I was finally free of that thing I had been begging the Lord to reveal. It was my root of Rejection, which had become such an unwelcome, toxic best friend in my life.

The next day, I stood in line to receive prayer. As to confirm His healing even more, the Lord used another woman to verbally encourage me. I was paired with a pastor who did not know a single thing about me. She placed her hands on me and began to pray. She stopped mid-sentence, looked me straight in the eyes and delivered a powerful prophetic word, "God has called you for a very specific purpose. You are a force to be reckoned with. You tick the enemy off the minute your feet hit the ground in the morning. You have felt like something is wrong with you. God was not waiting on you to 'act better' or 'do more.' He was waiting for you to be healed of a deep wound. God's call for you will scare you, and there will be obstacles. But God has given you everything you need to fulfill His purpose. The time is now."

I knew the Lord was speaking right to my heart through her. I floated out of church feeling confident God made a clear point. It was finished. I was healed, and I felt certain it was time to walk out God's call, whatever it may be.

THE ONLY BLOOD THAT MATTERS

During this season of my life, my husband traveled frequently and was usually gone throughout the week. I had a lot of extra time on my hands in the evenings after the kids went to bed. My curiosity about my potential additional family got the best of me, so I began a little investigation. I searched on Google People Search and Facebook. I immediately found what I thought was John's family, the Prestons. It seemed that John and Nancy were still married and lived close to me. I found a Wendy Michelle. She was married with a son. To my added surprise, there was another Preston, a thirty-two-year-old man named Luke. Personally, I didn't think any of them looked like me, so I began doubting they were my relatives.

During this time I prayed fervently, "God, lead me. Don't let me do anything that is not Your will. Stop me in my tracks if I am not supposed to be searching for these people."

Late one night I sat down with my computer again, mindlessly searching for any information on the Prestons. I was searching the same two websites, looking at pictures and trying to piece together any information I could uncover. All of a sudden, my computer screen went black. Two inch, bold, red letters moved horizontally across my screen:

WARNING. WARNING. A VIRUS IS TRYING TO ATTACK YOUR COMPUTER.

My eyes widened and my heart raced! I called my husband. He inquired about the websites I was surfing. I assured him that the only two websites I visited were Google People Search and Facebook. He said, "Turn the computer off and go to bed. I think you have your answer."

The next day, I turned on the computer, and there was nothing wrong with it. I sat there in awe because it appeared God wanted my attention. It was as though He said, "Get off the computer and put down your search, sweet daughter. I've got this."

He inserted something in my spirit that would be the ultimate truth to which I clung during the next part of this journey, "Freddie is your daddy. You do share the same blood. It's My blood, the only blood that matters."

I exhaled softly as I put my computer away. I knew now that the Lord wanted me to surrender my questions and trust Him. I didn't know it at the time, but I was embarking upon an adventure that would require full confidence in God and His plan, and I needed this anchor in my soul.

WHAT MATTERS

You may have heard someone say, "Get to the root of it!" What they mean is, tell me where it started. When did it happen for the first time? Get to the point! If we only treat symptoms of the heart and fail to address the underlying causes, we will spend a lifetime struggling to place faulty bandage after faulty bandage over the wounds of our heart. But God's desire for us is a complete healing, not a temporary fix.

To look at it another way, let's use a gardening analogy. We can spend all day cutting weeds out of our yard, and they grow right back. It is only when we take the time and intention to dig down deep, tug a little harder, and pull out the entire weed, roots and all, that we can finally ensure it won't grow back. I spent years tugging on my weeds using my own strength. But the instant the root was revealed, God completed the process for good. He does that.

FIND THE ROOT

Is there an area in your life that's littered with weeds? Have you prayed and asked God to reveal the exact moment the weeds entered your life? Stop and ask God now. Allow Him to reveal the root. Then ask Him to remove it, and believe by faith it is gone.

I'm fully convinced Satan introduced the horror of abortion because of its traumatic negative effects. Some of you have had an abortion, some of you may have considered it, and some of you may have almost been aborted. God is in the business of healing and forgiving. Let God heal these places. Receive His healing and forgiveness, and forgive yourself.

Chapter Ten

BLOOD DOES MATTER

It took only weeks for me to understand why God halted my potential search for the truth.

NOT MY DADDY, TOO

My dad started to lose weight dramatically. It was too fast to be due to his recently disciplined eating habits. In addition to his rapid weight loss, he was constantly fatigued and felt persistent pain in his abdomen. In August of 2011, he finally made an appointment. The doctor performed a sonogram on my dad during that visit. They discovered a large mass in his abdomen. They immediately ordered a biopsy.

I was out of town the day my dad was supposed to hear his biopsy's results. I was visiting one of my friends, Rachel, in Houston when I received another dreadful phone call. As I answered my phone, I motioned for her to watch our collective seven kids because I needed privacy. I ran outside and said a quick prayer for good news. My mom's voice shook,

"The results came back from the biopsy. Your dad has cancer. They think it is pancreatic cancer. Honey, the doctor doesn't think he will have much longer."

Her shock was made apparent by the lack of emotion in her voice. But my mind sped around the consequences of what my mom told me.

Wait. What did she say? Not much longer for what? Surely she isn't saying he doesn't have much longer to live.

Miraculously, I held it together. Partly to appear strong for my mom, but mostly because I was in utter shock. It was as though I was in a tunnel again, hearing this strange voice say this awful thing. But I couldn't even comprehend it. She said that *word*, that dreaded, awful word. My sweet daddy had cancer. The worst kind. The deadly kind.

I wish I could tell you some spiritually-moving story about how I fell to my knees in prayer, believing he was going to be healed. But nope. I hung up and did what any daddy's girl would do. I ran around to the back of Rachel's house so no one could hear me and collapsed into the fetal position, screaming and crying. A moan escaped from my lips that came from the core of who I was. It was a sound similar to the one my soul released on the night I lost my Bub. It appeared my heart didn't have enough energy left to lose someone else. The emotional turmoil resulting from all the traumatic events I experienced so close together stacked on top of my lungs like bricks, making it difficult to breathe.

Just breathe.

I don't know how long I spent on the ground, but I eventually gathered my composure enough to go inside and tell Rachel the news. I suppose my outer appearance reflected my inner distress, because I didn't even have to say a word. Standing at her kitchen island, she took one look at my splotchy face and mangled hair and knew. She shook her head and cried, "No, Dana! No!"

I collapsed into her arms as our tears mingled. I wanted to get to my dad as soon as possible. Once again, I would have been a danger to myself and society had I gotten behind the wheel of my vehicle. I was too distraught to drive the four hours home. As soon as I called my husband to give him the news, his mind was made up. He boarded the next flight to Houston to drive me and the kids home safely. I wasn't emotionally or mentally capable of picking my husband up from the airport. When his plane landed, I literally drove around for hours trying to find the airport! Poor Rachel! I called her several times in tears, asking for directions. I felt lost. I was lost in more ways than one. She tried to remain calm because, well, one of us needed to be sane. She could tell I was on the verge of a mental breakdown. By the grace of God, I finally found the airport and managed to crawl into the passenger seat, letting my husband take the wheel. We made it back to Rachel's in half the time it should have taken.

That night, Rachel was an angel, tending to all the children. She told my husband and me to spend some time alone outside. Her backyard is a true oasis, and we felt like we were at a resort. Scott and I put on our swimsuits and got into the pool. We swam over to the grotto in her pool and looked up at the stars. I tried to talk about what life would be like without my daddy. I kept repeating, "I can't believe this. I can't believe this."

My tears came intermittently that night. My husband cried, too. The water was soothing. The stars assured us of God's existence. There in the water, a peace that passes all understanding eventually washed over me. A calmness enveloped me, and I was able to go to sleep soundly that night.

The next morning, we were up with the sun. We gave our hugs, said our goodbyes, and hit the road. I braced myself for what would be waiting for us at home. I thought of my mom and dad and the changes we were all about to experience yet again.

Along Highway I35, somewhere between Waco and Alvarado, my phone rang. It was my mom, and she was absurdly, inappropriately happy.

"Dana, the doctor was wrong! He spoke before they received the results of all the tests. Your dad does not have pancreatic cancer, but non-Hodgkin's lymphoma! It is a very treatable and highly curable cancer!"

Every emotion shuffled through my heart in a matter of ten seconds! Waves of heat rolled through my entire my body. For twenty-four long, painful hours, I thought my dad was going to die. And in an instant, my mind shifted to ensuring my dad would live. These feelings were eerily familiar, as we had experienced them with my mom's diagnosis only a few years before.

Later, we learned the doctor prematurely diagnosed pancreatic cancer because of the location of the mass. He spoke before receiving the particular tissue sample test to reveal the exact form of cancer. So yes, my dad switched doctors. I think he said something along the lines of, "Over my living body will I let you oversee my health!"

The next six months revolved around my dad's health and treatment. I spent my time taking him to chemo appointments, doctors' appointments, and radiation appointments. In February of 2012, he was in remission! All cancer was gone from my dad's body. Gratitude abounded.

THE DAY THAT CHANGED EVERYTHING

Throughout all the chaos of taking care of a cancer patient, our family was spending a lot of time at my parents' house. One afternoon we were hanging out there with my Nantie. Nothing was out of the ordinary. We were chatting casually when one conversation literally altered my life.

My dad walked into the room and thought aloud, "I can't wait for this chemo to get out of my body so I can start giving blood again."

I laughed. "That is the weirdest thing to say, Dad. Who enjoys giving blood?!"

He proudly defended his excitement. "I'm a universal donor! I have Type O blood."

My smile faded. My fingers tingled. My stomach churned. I turned to my mom, "Mom, I thought you were type O blood?"

She answered without hesitation, "I am Type O."

Settling into his favorite chair, my dad asked, "Why, what type are you?"

I had learned my blood type when I gave birth to my children, and I never forgot it. My answer was so simple, yet carried such profound weight. It was one letter, but its consequences were innumerable.

"I'm Type A."

If alarms aren't sounding off in your mind right now, reach back in your brain and revisit your junior high science lessons. That's precisely what I did in that moment. I couldn't recall all the various blood type combinations, but I remembered there was something very unique about two Type O parents.

As quickly as it started, the blood type conversation ended. Nothing else was mentioned. Someone else started on a new topic. No one seemed bothered.

I, on the other hand, was numb. The continued conversation muffled as I attempted to maintain a normal composure. I sat still in my chair. I tried to control my breathing. As calmly as I could, I reached for my phone and searched for a blood typing chart. I clicked on the American Red Cross website. I scrolled past information about recipients vs. donors and blood type population and landed on the section labeled: How Is My Blood Type Determined?

Yes. That's what I was looking for.

My eyes darted frantically across the chart, finally locating the "O" column. The rest of the webpage blurred. My eyes couldn't compute information to my brain fast enough. Time froze. There, on my tiny screen, were the words "O+O=only O."

My heart kept beating though I felt like it stopped. I was grateful to be sitting in a chair as my head grew foggy. I stared at the screen, re-reading and re-confirming what I knew in my heart to be true. But I didn't want to make a mistake. I wanted to be sure. A huge part of me was shocked and in disbelief that my questions could have been answered so easily!

All we had to do was compare blood types? How could we have not known? But deep down, I knew it all along.

This is why I never had a peace.

This is why I always questioned my truth.

This is why the doubts and wonders never left me.

This is why I could never shake the feelings.

This is why I could never be settled.

Because I didn't think it was the appropriate time to shout what I just discovered, I quietly excused myself to the restroom. I stepped into the bathroom and locked the door. I looked in the mirror, allowing my face to reflect how I was feeling but didn't have the freedom to make in the other room.

My eyes widened, my jaw dropped. I gasped as I thought, "Are you kidding me?"

I bent over and splashed some cool water on my face. I took a moment to gather myself before leaving. I walked out of the bathroom but remained in the back of the house near the bedrooms. I waited and hoped my husband or aunt would need to use the restroom soon. It wasn't long before I saw my aunt walking down the hall. I motioned for her to hurry up and come to me. She looked confused, but obliged. I pulled her into a bedroom and whisper-shouted, "John is my bio-logical father! Did you hear that conversation? My dad and mom are both Type O blood. I am an A. Two Type O parents can only have a Type O child!"

Taken aback, she asked, "Wait. What? What do you *mean*? How do you know?"

I had to repeat the details a few more times until it sank in. She was clearly dazed and muddled. It actually wasn't great news for her. I think she immediately realized this meant she and I didn't share the same blood either. Still wrapping her head around this revelation, she asked, "Well, what are you going to do?"

"I have no idea."

I decided not to spill the beans that day. It was not the right time. The house was full of people. I wanted to talk to my husband first. This could wait another day.

The rest of the day was a total blur, and I don't really recall anything else I said or did. It was surreal to think that in all my life, throughout all my questioning, all we had to do to find answers was compare blood types! In the midst of a simple conversation, I realized that so many things about my life were a lie. Not a lie someone had told to deceive me, but a lie I believed my entire life. The truth? Freddie, my daddy, was not my biological father.

WHAT MATTERS

One of the biggest lessons I learned during this particular season of loss and near loss is that we really don't have much control. We try to direct our lives down certain paths, but at the end of the day, there are outside influences that we cannot always foresee or alter.

Most of us have received unexpected news. Some of us have been wrecked by news we received. Some of us have allowed the news to make us stronger. When faced with life altering news, we have a decision to make. Will we let it make us bitter or better?

FIND THE ROOT

Oh, the moments when O+O doesn't add up! Have you had moments when things in your life don't quite add up to what you expected? Did you assume that one action + another action would obviously result in your expected outcome? God's ways are beyond our understanding. He has a plan more fantastic than our own! If something is not adding up in your life like you expected, it may be time to let go, let God take the wheel, and trust Him.

In what areas of your life do you need God to provide a healthy perspective? How can He help you change your view of a certain situation? Where might you be believing a lie?

Sometimes, it's simply about surrendering the outcome to God. "He is a faithful God, who keeps his promises and is merciful to thousands of generations" (Deuteronomy 7:9). We don't always receive the outcomes we want or think we need, but our attitude can change everything!

Chapter Eleven

BLOOD IS NOT ALWAYS THICKER THAN WATER

A couple of days passed after the blood type discovery. I struggled with the best course of action now that I possessed this information. I contemplated how I was going to relay this news to my parents. On top of that, I was still letting the truth marinate in my own heart and mind. How *does* one process that the dad who raised them is not their biological father? "Process" became my theme word. Everything happened in a process, and each step required major mental and emotional work.

I spent these days talking the ears off my husband and closest friends. I had a handful of close friends who knew I dealt with these burning questions throughout my life. They knew I longed for answers, but that I didn't know how to get them. They were stunned when I called to explain that a simple conversation revealed the truth. There was a sense of shock and apprehension amongst all of us. No one gave me advice regarding my next move. I didn't ask for it, but

I'm also sure they didn't know *how* to advise me! This was uncharted territory for all of us. We shared a quiet sense of disbelief and astonishment. We knew God was the only one who could guide me through such a difficult circumstance.

The weekend after the blood type conversation, I picked up the phone and called my aunt. I wondered if she heard anything from my parents. I needed to know if the truth also struck my parents. I needed to know how to approach the conversation with them. My aunt told me that my mom had been crying for two days. During our discussion, my mom was also able to put two and two together. I honestly can't believe we both managed to stay so calm in the middle of the subtle explosion! I think the Holy Spirit played a huge role. When I finished my conversation with my aunt, I decided to go to my parents' house, and I needed to go alone. I wanted to talk to my mom first. I wanted to check on her and find out how my dad was handling the news. I waited until the following Monday afternoon before my dad got home from work.

Monday arrived and brought with it a heap of anxiety. I felt sick. I dreaded confronting the information. I dreaded my mother's reaction and worried about her heart. I dreaded hearing about my dad and how he was dealing with the news. I knew the initial conversation would be the most difficult. Along with an army of prayer warriors, I was praying for both myself and my parents. Even though I was riddled with nerves, a supernatural confidence rose in me. I knew this would be the hardest part, and I just wanted to get past it. I wanted to get this conversation over with, and with God's grace, I knew I could do it.

I called my mom and let her know I needed to swing by and speak her. It was evident she knew something because she didn't question why I was coming. When I arrived at my parents' house that afternoon, my mom was sitting in her favorite chair, waiting for me. I walked in, hugged her, and sat down in a chair across the room. Getting right to the point, I spoke about our earlier conversation. Before I could finish, she admitted she realized the truth in that moment, too. Tears filled her eyes as she stumbled over apologies. "I am so sorry! I really didn't know. I truly thought Dad was your dad. I wasn't lying, and I was always honest with everyone."

I assured her of my understanding. I truly believed her. I asked how my dad took the news.

"He doesn't know. He didn't catch it. I'm not sure how to tell him. Do you want to be the one to tell him?"

I didn't even have to think about it, "Yes, I want to be the one to tell him." I wanted to break the news as simply and tenderly as possible.

My mom and I talked for a while before my dad got home from work. At one point, my mom left the room. I'm not sure if she really just needed a restroom break or if she needed a moment alone. After a few minutes, I stood up and went to look for her. I met my mom in the hallway as she was coming out of the bathroom. My short mom approached me and wrapped her arms around my waist. We held each other for a moment and cried. I felt like a mother comforting her child, our roles were reversed. As I held her, I could sense a release of emotions. I thought I sensed guilt, shame, regret, and shock.

She looked up and humbly asked, "Will you please forgive me?"

Through tears, my response was quick and honest. "Mom, I have already forgiven you. Now you are going to have to forgive yourself!"

In an instant I forgave her and it was a done deal. A part of me felt like there wasn't anything to forgive. I knew she just needed to say it. Her true struggle was going to be forgiving herself. Sadly, we forgive others more quickly than we forgive ourselves. We are often our own biggest roadblocks to freedom. I already received some deep freedom in the last six months, and I felt as though I should freely give what I freely received. I didn't want to hold anything against anyone involved in this situation. Looking back, I felt the Lord waited for me to be free of Rejection before he revealed the truth. It caused me to enter into this season with so much more peace and grace to offer everyone involved.

My mom and I walked back to the den to wait for my dad. I heard the front door creak as it opened. Like clockwork, I observed my dad's evening rhythm of storing away his items in the secretary desk before he entered the living room. When he saw me sitting with my mom, his face lit up with excitement. But it didn't take him long to realize something was wrong. His face grew serious when he saw our tear-stained faces. He hugged and kissed my mom and then me. I asked him to sit down. I took a deep breath to settle my nerves and began.

"Dad, do you remember the other day when we were here, and we talked about our blood types?"

He looked perplexed. "Yes?"

"You said you were Type O, and Mom said she was Type O. I also told you that I am Type A. Well, I looked on the blood type chart, and two O parents can only have an O child."

I paused to let it sink in. I hoped I didn't need to connect the dots for him. I didn't.

Picking his jaw up off the floor, he exclaimed, "Well I'll be!"

I can still see the shock on his face as he turned from me to face my mom. Mom fell apart, "I'm sorry, Freddie. I really didn't know! I promise I really thought she was yours!"

For a moment, they entered their own conversation, together trying to determine how this happened. My mom was super emotional and my dad was purely shocked. He wasn't mad, he was just gut-punched. He is a pretty calm, steady guy anyway. It was possible he was experiencing a million emotions on the inside, but we would never know. After a few minutes, my dad scooted to the edge of his seat and looked straight at me.

Meeting his eyes, I felt the emotion in the words that emerged from the tenderest part of his heart, "You are my girl. You are my girl! That won't ever change. You are mine!" True to his character, his concern wasn't for himself, but for me. "How are you? How are you doing?"

I emphatically assured him, "I am fine, Dad. This changes nothing. You are my daddy, and that will never change!"

In this moment, blood did *not* matter. This man raised me. He had been my daddy for nearly forty years. And being a daddy is so much more than sharing DNA. *He* was the one who tucked me into bed at night. *He* was the one who read all the *Raggedy Ann and Andy* books to me. *He* was the one who worked his entire life to provide a life for me. *He* was the one at my graduations. *He* was the one who walked me down the aisle.

Echoing one another's sentiments, he reiterated, "You are my daughter, and those babies are my grandkids!" He repeated the last part of that sentence several times. He wanted it to be clear.

You see, my brother and sister never had any kids of their own. I often joked that I did my part to populate the earth and continue the family. So my four kids are my parents' only grandchildren. And while it was important to my dad that I realize this revelation would change nothing between us, it was equally important for my dad to remind me that it would change nothing between him and his grandkids. He was PaPa. Period. Until this moment, I never considered the fact that my dad did not share blood with five of the most important people in his life: me and my four children.

I was relieved the information was out in the open and that this initial conversation was almost over. I was emotionally and mentally drained. I know my mom was, too. At the end of our conversation, my dad turned to me and asked, "So what are you going to do?"

I had been so consumed with figuring out how to tell my parents that I hadn't considered the next step. I told him I wasn't sure, but I would pray and seek God's will.

I laughed when he said, "Well, I wouldn't want to be in your shoes."

We wrapped up our conversation. I assumed my parents needed some time alone. I gave my hugs and said my goodbyes. My dad didn't want to be in my shoes, but neither did I.

WHAT IF?

My story was the topic of many conversations. My friends jokingly called and asked, "How are the The Days of Dana's Life going?"

I've been blessed with some rock-solid friendships in my life. I believe my friends had my best interest in their hearts. Throughout these conversations, my friends always inquired about my plans. It wasn't because they were nosey; they truly cared and really wanted to know about my life. But I had no concrete answer for them. I was wondering about the same things they were. In their concern, my friends also presented many aspects to consider:

What if John and Nancy's marriage isn't strong enough to handle this information?

What if Nancy had no clue John was dating your mother and it ends their marriage?

What if it is too much for your new brother and sister to handle?

What if…what if?

SEEKING MY SISTER

It was Easter 2012, and we were headed to my aunt's house. My sister, Shawna, was off work for the day and would be in attendance at this family function. I was very thankful and eager to see her. I hoped she would not back out at the last minute as she had in the past. Shawna was still clueless about our life-changing discovery. I did not think a phone call was appropriate for this kind of conversation, so I waited until I could tell her in person. My mom respected my request to save the conversation for me and my sister first. This is the day I would get my chance to talk to Shawna.

After lunch, I asked Shawna to come outside so we could talk. We walked out on the back porch and made ourselves comfortable at the patio table. I told her about my questioning over the years and my uncertainty about Dad being my biological father. It was something she and I had never discussed before. It was all news to her. The story unfolded, ending with the conclusion that Dad was not my biological father. My sister handled the news just as graciously as I anticipated, maybe even more so. By the look on her face, I was able to peg the moment she realized this meant she and I did not share the same blood.

She looked me squarely in the face and said, "You're my sister, and this changes nothing between us!"

I agreed and repeated the declaration back to her. Once again, blood didn't matter. We grew up together. We shared the same daddy. We were sisters.

I explained that, through a little investigation, I found all the Prestons. She was amazed by how close everyone lived. We scrolled through social media to take a peek at my new family. With a huge smile she said, "So you have another sister and brother! Are you going to meet them?"

I quickly rattled off all the excuses behind my uncertainty. I mumbled on about some potentially negative scenarios and shrugged my shoulders.

She wasn't buying it.

"Wait. How could you not? You have another brother and sister! How could you not meet them? I couldn't live my life without you as my sister, and they have a right to know you are their sister, too!"

Her point of view changed everything for me. Leave it to a sister to tell you how it really is! A light switched on in my mind and I held my head higher. She was right. I had another brother and sister. How could I not know them?

God used my sister to shift my thinking. It seemed that everyone else viewed my story from Freddie's, Lana's, Nancy's, and John's positions. She was the first person who observed things entirely from my point of view. She spoke to my sister-heart, the very thing that accelerated my search for answers. I left the conversation feeling loved. However, one question plagued my mind: how was I going to tell Luke and Wendy that I was their long-lost sister?

WHAT MATTERS

Blessed are we who live in a world full of adoptive families! Sharing the same blood has become irrelevant. In a world full of division and separation, loving people enough to make them a part of our family is one of the greatest ways we can bring the love of God to a broken society.

Scott and I have friends who feel more like family than some of our actual family. We're lucky to have people in our lives who invite us into the depths of who they are, even allowing us to see the messiest parts of their hearts and lives. And as you know from my story, we are blessed in return by their generosity in times of chaos and despair. My kids adore our friends and look to them as their aunts and uncles. I'm convinced it is love that makes a family. Not DNA. Not blood.

FIND THE ROOT

How often do you forgive others faster than you forgive yourself? Extend some grace to yourself today! How can you finally release guilt or shame and forgive yourself?

In what ways do you need to be honest with yourself, even if it means digging up truths you would rather keep hidden?

What game-changing moments have you experienced? Reflect on them. Write them down as important moments on your spiritual timeline. Journal the experiences as monuments to the power of change in your life.

Chapter Twelve

SISTER, SISTER

After much prayer and thought, I felt the Lord remind me of His Word in John 8:32, "…and you will know the truth, and the truth will set you free." I felt that as long as only my family knew the truth, it was only *half* true. It wouldn't be entirely true until everyone knew.

LETTERS AND LONGING

I prayed hard for John, Nancy, Wendy, and Luke. As much as the news would impact them all, I knew John was about to receive the greatest shock of all. At seventy years old, he was going to learn he had another thirty-nine-year-old daughter. Wendy and I were only two months apart. John would realize he had missed thirty-nine years of his daughter's life. He would discover that he had four biological grandchildren.

I decided to write Wendy a letter first. Thanks to modern technology, it wasn't hard to find her address (she lived just five minutes from me). As I prepared my letter, my mom told me she would like to write to John before I sent my letter to Wendy. It was her story to tell John, and she thought he should find out before his daughter. That sounded reasonable to me, and I quickly agreed. I'd feel the same if I was in her shoes. I asked her to include a few sentences at the end of her letter to John, making it clear that Wendy would be receiving a letter from me in two weeks. Two weeks would give him ample time to process the information and grant him the opportunity to tell his wife and two grown children.

Over the next few days, my mom composed her letter to John. She is an amazing writer, so I knew she would write a great letter. I also knew her main struggle would be keeping it succinct. I encouraged her to leave out any emotion and stick to relaying the facts. After editing, we cut her five-page letter down to one-and-a-half pages!

My letter rested, written, on my desk for weeks, waiting to be sent. I assumed my mom sent hers out, and I was just giving John the time we promised. That evening, my mom called me. I was in the car with my family, driving home from church. I answered with the small hope she may have received a response to her letter. On the contrary, she informed me that she hadn't sent the letter, and she wasn't going to. As I pressed her, my mom admitted it was my dad who decided he did not want my mom to contact John. I didn't blame him. John wasn't my dad's favorite person, as he technically dated his wife back in 1972. My dad was wrestling with confusing emotions. He just received the blow of a lifetime. His baby girl was another man's biological daughter. That other man just happened to be John. I think a little anger and jealousy led him to prohibit his wife from sending the letter.

Up until this point, I handled everything pretty rationally considering the circumstances. I could feel the prayer support from my close friends, because by nature, I am not always cool and collected. When I am cool and collected, you know it is God working in me. My personality is energetic, and I usually approached situations with more passion, to put it kindly. I knew this situation was a lot to digest for everyone, so I made a point to keep things as peaceful as possible, always being aware of others' feelings. But this? This pushed me over the edge.

I dropped my family off at home and took a spin around the block. Since my brother's death, my car was often my safe place to vent. So I pressed the gas and called my mom again. It was the first time I raised my voice throughout this entire process. Bottom line, I felt like I had been abandoned in this mess. Yes, this news was big, but it was a direct result of choices they made, yet they were choosing to let me deal with it alone.

Rejection roared, eager to get another shot at me; but this time, I roared back.

"I disagree with you and Dad! I think you should send the letter. This is not my fault! I feel like you and Dad are leaving me for dead. We just discovered this massive piece of information and you are washing your hands of it? You are just leaving me to handle everything? I think that's wrong!"

My dad's heart changed in a matter of seconds. I think hearing my passion on the phone took him by surprise. He was unaware I thought the letter held such importance. I heard him stammer in the background, "Okay, okay! Tell her you will send the letter!"

My passion subsided as my mom agreed, with the permission of my dad, to send the letter the next day.

I patiently waited two weeks before I sent Wendy's letter. In the meantime, I conducted a little investigative work. I wanted to be sure we had the correct address for John's house. Since he lived less than ten miles from me, I drove by a few times. As only God could orchestrate, one of the times I drove by, John was standing in his front yard. I recognized him immediately from all the nighttime Facebook stalking, I mean, *searching*, I'd performed months ago. I assured my mom her letter went to the correct address. If we didn't get a response, we didn't want to wonder if it made it into the correct hands.

John received his letter, but he did not share it with his daughter, Wendy. Her revelation arrived in the mail the Friday before Memorial Day in May 2012. I sent the letter, praying it would be received with grace and love. I also drove by her house one day out of curiosity. To my surprise, I saw her husband and son in their big front window! I was relieved that we had the correct address for her, too. I waited anxiously for her to read the words I penned so carefully and lovingly:

May 22, 2012

Wendy,

I have known about you for as long as I can remember. I have been praying for many months that God would prepare you and your family for the news you were given. At this point, I am assuming your mom and dad told you about the letter they received in the mail from my mom.

In case not, my name is Dana Michelle (Wagnon) Sellars. My mom, Lana Wagnon, dated your father back in 1971-72. Without going into great detail, and to keep from dishonoring anyone, Lana and John were dating while "supposedly" divorcing their current spouses. However, they both continued to see their spouses, while still seeing each other.

Your mom, Nancy, and my mom, Lana, ended up pregnant within a few months of each other. I was born December 31, 1972 and I know you were born a few months before. When my mom found out she was pregnant, she was convinced I belonged to my dad, Freddie. All the while, the possibility of John being my biological father was in the back of everyone's minds. As my mom shared in her letter to your parents, through medical circumstances, we found out through blood that my dad, Freddie, cannot be my biological father. So your father is the only other man it could be.

I can't imagine the shock and emotions your family has gone through the last few weeks. I have known of this possibility as long as I can remember and I bet you had no clue. For this reason, I have been fervently praying for everyone in your family, especially your mom. I want you to know I'm a believer in Jesus Christ. I know God is mighty to heal the deepest secrets and the most painful wounds. I searched for you on Facebook and assumed, by your interests, that you're a believer, too! For that reason, I'm hopeful you will turn to God for comfort and healing as you process this information.

I have to tell you my purpose for writing you, as my mom and I debated taking this information to the grave. But that option did not settle in my soul. God makes it clear in His Word to bring things to the light, and the truth is what sets you free. So for just our family to know this is only revealing half the truth. I thought it was only fair if everyone knew the facts. I don't write because I need a dad, God gave me the perfect daddy. I can only hope and believe that God gave you the perfect daddy in John. I know one thing for sure: God works all plans out for His good.

I have been praying that God would ultimately take care of all of us and for His will to be done in this situation. I really want what is best for everyone. If the truth coming out is as far as it goes, then I've done what I felt God wanted me to do. I would be open to meeting you, but I'm preparing my heart for the fact that it may not happen. Not only are we half-sisters, but we are sisters in Christ.

I hope you know that I never wanted to hurt anyone. I have such a heart for everyone, but especially for Nancy. I didn't know how much she knew or how much of this is new information. I am fervently praying that this doesn't cause huge damage and that we all lean on a good God to get us through. Although I don't know you, God has given me a love for you and Luke. I truly believe God works for the good of those who love Him and who have been called to His purpose.

In Him,
Dana Sellars

SUBSEQUENT SURPRISES

That Monday night, my family was at a friend's house celebrating Memorial Day. As we sat around a table by their pool, my phone sounded with a Facebook update. I clicked on my Facebook app and read "Wendy Reed has requested your friendship on Facebook."

I gasped and shared the news with my friends. Expressing my exact thoughts, my friend Maria said, "Dana, this means she believes you!"

I jumped up when I saw a private message from Wendy. I ran in the house as my heart pounded and began reading.

Dana,

I received your letter in the mail on Saturday. We have been in East Texas for the holiday weekend with my husband's family so it has taken me a couple days to respond. Thank you for your sweet letter and the picture of you and your precious family. I would love to meet you and talk with you sometime. My phone number, if you would like to call, is (555)234-1298. I don't always hear it ring, but if you send me a text or leave a voicemail I will check it and get back to you. I knew my parents had some issues during that time so some things were new information (you :)) and some were not. I am a Christian and appreciate your prayers for my family. God bless all of you.

In Christ,
Wendy

I must have read her message five times! I thought, "She had a smiley face when she said I was new information, so surely she was not devastated about the news."

I immediately texted Wendy and asked if we could talk soon.

She responded quickly, "I'm available now".

I told her I would call her as soon as I got home. On the way home, my stomach churned with a nervous excitement as I thought about how our conversation might flow. I ran into the house, locked myself in my bedroom, and made the call.

First things first. I wanted to explain who I was and how I could possibly be her sister. I shared my parent's story. After a long pause, Wendy said, "I want to be honest from the start.

My dad was not the only one seeing someone else in 1972. So, I may not be your sister, but Luke would be your brother."

Silly me, thinking all the surprises were over. My mind went blank. I legitimately didn't understand what she was saying. She explained that while her dad was seeing my mom, her mom was seeing another man. She thinks that man might be her biological father. Wendy had been living with the same underlying question: do I have a different biological father?

After the initial shock wore off, we simply shared facts about our lives. Ironically, for a year's time we not only attended the same church, but the same 12:30 p.m. church service. She lived just five minutes from my house in the next city. We had been in close proximity all these years. After our conversation, which lasted a few hours, I was bursting with excitement. My smile was uncontainable as I relived the conversation with my husband. The next step was now obvious.

Wendy and I wanted to meet.

WHAT MATTERS

Taking steps toward learning the truth or sharing a difficult truth with someone else can seem daunting. Holding the course of someone else's life in your own hands is intimidating and overwhelming. In these situations, I find it best to take counsel from those who know me and love me. First, I ask God what He would have me do. Then, I seek advice from my husband and my inner circle of friends who know me better than anyone else.

When you're confused, clarity often comes through prayer and conversation with people who truly have your best interest at heart. We aren't meant to live our lives or walk difficult paths alone. God gave us community for a reason.

FIND THE ROOT

What truth do you need to discover or uncover? Revealing the truth is always better than hiding it. No matter what pain it causes, no matter how it may hurt, it's always best to reveal the truth because God will set you free in the process. Ask God to walk with you through this.

Do your circumstances seem all-consuming, like you are the only one going through something like this? The enemy wants to isolate us and make us feel alone. One thing is certain: you are not alone! Even as bizarre and unique as my situation was, I literally had someone (my sister) going through the exact same thing at the exact same time! Let God remind you that you are never alone.

Chapter Thirteen

ONE SWAB OF THE CHEEK

Something I loved about Wendy was that she too felt the urgency to learn the whole truth as soon as possible. We first talked on a Monday night and we set up a meeting for two days later. I arrived at Starbucks a little before our seven o'clock meeting time, so I sat on a bench outside and waited. Wendy pulled up, parked, and exited her car. We immediately recognized each other from the pictures we had seen on Facebook. We happily collided with a big warm hello and a hug. It did feel awkward at first. There's no manual on meeting your sister for the first time at age thirty-nine. What are you supposed to say? How are you supposed to act? I wasn't even sure how to feel. We ordered our drinks and found a table in the corner.

The conversation and questions began as soon as we sat down. While it didn't feel forced, it was more like a mini-interrogation. We started with casual questions about life and family. As we shared more details, almost every question I ever had in life was answered. Wendy mentioned that John had surgery on his left knee. I thought that was a fun coincidence and said, "So did I!"

She clarified, "Yes, but it was because he ran track."

This is was one of many jaw-dropping similarities connected that night. Not only did we both run track, we were both sprinters known for our speed.

I told Wendy about how tan I used to get during the summers when I was younger. I told her people thought I was Mexican because I was so dark-skinned. She gasped and told me her dad's tan was always so dark that people would speak Spanish to him, too. The parallels became humorous.

At one point, Wendy looked at me and asked in a way which indicated she already knew the answer, "Are you left-handed?"

Chills rand down my spine, "Yep."

I never felt so checked out in all my life. It wasn't in a creepy way, but I could see the wheels turning in Wendy's head the entire time. I had no idea what was going through her mind and heart. She couldn't take her eyes off me. As she later explained, I reminded her of many people in her family. I not only looked like her dad but I also acted like her (our) grandmother. I reminded her of her (our) brother. It was in those moments she realized she was looking at her daddy's daughter.

As our conversation concluded, Wendy informed me that John wanted a DNA test performed before we went any further. I figured a DNA test would be mentioned, but it surprisingly irritated me. I understood John wanted to be sure, but since my family already knew, it felt like a waste of time and money. I told Wendy I would do one, but that I couldn't pay for it. She assured me that John did not expect any money from me. She looked at me and said, "After tonight, even though my dad wants a DNA test, I have no doubt you are his daughter."

Wendy went to her parents' house the next day to tell them about our meeting. She looked John in the eyes, holding his attention, and promised him, "Dad, there is no doubt she is your daughter!"

Fortunately, Nancy was not as shocked as John appeared. One thing was decided, the DNA tests were about to happen, and they would leave no more room for questioning.

AND THE TRUTH WILL SET YOU FREE

The world of DNA tests was all new to me. I soon learned there are plenty of DNA labs from which to choose. I selected somewhere close and made my appointment. We decided my mom would go with me. Right before the appointment, a question popped into my head, accompanied by a peculiar feeling about the potential results of this test. What if the test came back negative? Then what? I didn't want to be humiliated. I asked, "Mom, are you sure there is no other possible father?" She reassured me that John was the only option.

My mom gave her DNA sample along with mine. It wasn't because we were wondering if she was my mom (although the thought probably did cross my mind). Actually, the fact that she was my mom was my only certainty. They needed her DNA for a very specific reason. The swab from my mom's cheek provided her DNA. They then took her DNA and separated it from my DNA. This would allow them to determine exactly what DNA I received from my biological mother and exactly what DNA I received from my biological father. Thus only comparing the DNA of my dad to that of John. This process would leave no room for error. That brought me some relief.

Since we were all getting DNA tests, Wendy decided to get one, too. She didn't want to miss out on all the fun. Just like me, she wondered if the man her mom dated while her parents were separated was her biological father. She too wanted her childhood questions answered. We left the lab expecting to receive an email with the results in a week.

A few days later, I was at the water park with my friend, Marci, and our kids. We were lounging, watching our children play in the pool. I happened to be on a lawn chair near my pool bag and heard my phone buzz with a text. Casually, I dug through my bag to retrieve my phone. I saw it was a text from Wendy. I was not anticipating the facts delivered across my screen: "I am sad to say we are not sisters, but we share a cute little brother."

I frantically shouted to Marci, "Watch my kids! I have to call Wendy."

I quickly dialed Wendy as I paced the sidewalks of the water park. She answered immediately, as if expecting my call. The second she said hello, I said, "Don't ever text me important information like that. Pick up the phone and call me!"

She explained that the DNA lab had emailed her the results early. She stared at her computer screen and read, "Your test says, regarding Johnathan Alan Preston, the probability of paternity is 99.99998%. My test says the probability of paternity is 0%."

My thoughts and emotions overtook me. I couldn't keep up.

"If it isn't 100%, does that still mean there is still a chance that John is not my father?"

Although I already knew that John was my father, there was something about hearing the official results that caused a deep despondency to envelop me. I realized now that I couldn't undo the results. There was no turning back. There it was in black and white: Johnathan Alan Preston was my biological father.

In finding that we did not share the same blood, Wendy and I discovered that the daddies who raised us were not our biological fathers. We were walking out the same testimony at the exact same time. It was a very tender moment between us. I found it endearing that Wendy's biggest disappointment was that we weren't real sisters. Luckily for her, I was taught that we don't say "step" or "half" when referring to anyone. We are all just family.

While on the phone with Wendy, a wave of regret flooded my mind. "I'm so sorry. I kind of feel bad right now. I feel like it's my fault that you just got this news."

"Don't be sorry. If you had not searched for your truth, I would have never gotten mine."

The man Wendy now knew was her biological father was killed in a car accident when she was a baby. Since he was not alive, she couldn't search for him. And she knew John would not have agreed to a DNA test with her otherwise. Truthfully, he was okay with not knowing. This served as a perfect example of how freedom is contagious. It exemplified how truth is revealed when we shine a light on our junk. If I didn't pursue the truth about my origin, Wendy would still be questioning hers today. I quickly determined to change my mindset. I would not let the enemy condemn me again over the subject. Instead, I praised God for leading me on a journey to find my truth, which in turn led to Wendy's truth.

WHAT MATTERS

We are never alone. Even though we each have a unique story, I can guarantee someone has gone through something very similar. We are all connected by our experiences and are meant to relate to one another in sympathy and empathy through those experiences. The Bible even says Jesus Himself went through temptations and experienced emotions, just like us.

The enemy loves to isolate and make us feel alone. He will try to convince us that we are the only one going through what we are going through. Know this: he is a liar. When I acknowledged this trap and let myself be reminded that my sister was right beside me, it gave me confidence, courage, and hope for the future instead of despair and confusion.

FIND THE ROOT

Have you ever entered a circumstance in which you don't know how things will turn out? It can be frightening and bring up insecurities. Pray and ask God to enter into the situation with boldness. Ask Him to give you peace no matter the outcome.

Discovering truth can be the key to helping others discover their own truth. Freedom spreads. Truth is revealed when we shine a light on our junk. What junk in your life can be lifted to God's light? Ask God to help you see the truth. How can you change your mindset, refusing to let the enemy condemn you? What truth can you share with others to help them be victorious? It's only the truth you know that sets you free.

Chapter Fourteen

A FATHER'S ACCEPTANCE

I eagerly waited to see how this adventure would progress. During this time, I sorted through many mixed feelings. In the beginning, I had a fear of Rejection. I feared how my new family would receive me, or if they would. I quizzed God, "You didn't heal me of Rejection because I am about to be deeply rejected, did You?" I prepared for the worst. In fact, I prepared so much for the worst, I wasn't prepared at all when John and Nancy said they wanted to meet me. My fear shifted quickly to excitement and then nervousness.

MEETING MY JOHN

Finally, the day arrived. Since the DNA tests, Wendy was the communicator between all of us. John and I hadn't even spoken on the phone. We waited to meet in person. I dug through drawers in my home, locating a scrapbook with pictures of me throughout the years. I thought it might bring John joy to see a bit of my past, as well as my present. I assumed he felt like he missed out on my life. I thought a scrapbook might bridge the gap.

Wendy and I met beforehand. She was a security blanket for me. It brought me comfort to have her there. She matched my eagerness for this meeting, and we giggled together, like sisters do. I looked out the window of McAlister's Deli and caught sight of John and Nancy. He looked just like he did in the pictures I saw on Facebook. He was a tall, white-haired, older man. I'm not being unkind, but it was hard to believe he was my father, which is greatly due to the fact that my dad was fifty-nine years old and John was seventy years old. The anticipation grew as he walked in the door and spotted me for the first time. His greeting was the absolute opposite of Rejection. He wrapped his long, shaking arms around me in a full embrace. He cried immediately, which of course spread like wildfire to us girls. John squeezed me and kissed me on the forehead. Luckily, I'm an affectionate person. He was speaking my language.

Nancy's loving character was evident within the first few minutes of meeting her. She patiently waited her turn to welcome me with a warm embrace. There we were, in the middle of the restaurant, hugging and bawling. I'm sure we were a sight for the other patrons. We took our place in line, and for the first time, my biological father bought me something: lunch. He seemed so proud to treat me. We filled our drinks and chose a table in the corner, away from the crowd.

For the next several hours, we talked and talked and talked. I shared things I thought they would want to know. Nancy asked questions that stirred even more discussion. About halfway through our visit, I realized John hadn't spoken much. There was a time when he reached across the table and grabbed my hand. He started to say something, but his lip quivered. His emotions kept him from sharing. He simply kept patting my hand and crying.

I finally asked, "What is it? What are you trying to say? What are you thinking that is making you so emotional?"

He took my hands into his trembling hands and said, "I just hope you aren't disappointed."

I wanted to be clear, vulnerable, and understood, "Don't say that! How could I be disappointed in God's plan? The enemy wanted to destroy your marriage and he failed! The enemy wanted to destroy my parents' marriage and he failed. The enemy wanted to destroy Wendy and me with all of this and he failed! I could never be disappointed with how God worked things out for good!"

John responded with a little nod of his head. I wasn't sure what it meant, but I was confident he believed me. Looking back, I think he may have actually meant something deeper. The more comfortable we became with one another over time, the more we would encounter the other's negative characteristics. I now understand that he feared my disappointment in him.

Toward the end of our lunch, my new family called my little brother Luke. Living many states away, he wondered how things were going. They handed me the phone and said, "Here, talk to him." It felt bizarre, I must admit. What was I supposed to say?

Uncomfortably, I accepted the phone and starting talking with hesitation. During our conversation, he volunteered, "If you ever want to come to New York, I have a place. We could meet." I wasn't sure if he was sincere, but I tucked that piece of information in the back of my mind, just in case.

After our lunch, they asked if I wanted to visit my new cousin's gift shop down the street so I could meet more family. John's older brother and his wife worked there and they were anxious to meet me. As we pulled into the parking lot, I recognized the shop instantly. It was a shop I visited on multiple occasions in the past. In fact, when I walked in and met my new aunt and uncle, I realized I had met them before. What a small world! I looked around their shop and found a little wooden sign that read, "If God brings you to it, He will bring you through it." I brought it up to the counter and said, "Well I guess I have to buy this sign after all this."

My sweet Aunt Kristy said, "Put your wallet away. Consider this our 'welcome to the family' gift!"

We visited for a while. They mentioned how much I reminded them of John when he was younger. I reminded them of Luke as well. We hugged, said our goodbyes, and went our separate ways.

WHAT ABOUT THE GRANDKIDS?

When I turned the ignition, I felt a burning desire to call the first man I ever loved: my daddy. I couldn't imagine how he was feeling right now, sitting at home, knowing I was out to lunch with John. He was kind and asked me how everything transpired.

I said, "Dad, you have nothing to worry about. I don't think I will feel like John is a dad."

"Oh yeah, why is that?"

"Well, he is much older than you, and I am used to having a young dad However, I am sure I will feel related to him. I could see him feeling like my family, but you will always be my only daddy."

My dad seemed to take solace in the sentiment. See, I always had the youngest dad amongst all my friends. The age difference between my dad and John, then, relieved any possible sense of competition. It was important to me that my dad knew he holds a place in my heart that no other man can hold.

I walked in the house and dropped my purse on the ground. I looked at my husband, who was sitting on the couch, and said, "Well, I have a whole new family if I want it."

As the words left my mouth, I considered something I hadn't before: John and Nancy would want to meet my kids. Of *course* they would want to meet *their* grandkids! But I had not thought this far in advance. I was just trying to get through writing a letter, the first phone conversations, and meeting them myself. My heart sank as I realized I needed to figure out how to explain this to my kids. As I rehearsed conversations in my mind, I couldn't help but think about how this might sit with my parents.

A few days after meeting John and Nancy, my dad was at my house to bring my kids home from a fun day out. I asked the kids to stay inside as I walked him to his car. I wanted to see if I could get a good sense of how he was feeling. During our chat, I looked at him and said, "Dad, there is something I want to tell you. John wants to meet the grandkids."

He responded with a selfless, "Okay. I don't blame him. If I knew I had four grandkids out there, I would want to meet them, too."

I was surprised by his response. I was expecting more hesitation. But it was the one I needed to hear. Without knowing it, my dad gave me permission and released me for the inevitable meeting. My four kids, his only four grandchildren, were going to meet their new grandparents. My parents were going to have to share them.

WHAT MATTERS

The kindness and graciousness with which everyone handled this unique situation will never cease to amaze me. Where there could have been closed doors, acceptance was chosen. Where there could have been pride, humility was chosen. Where there could have been hurt or betrayal, healing and loyalty were chosen. We all find ourselves in situations that demand similar choices from us. We can choose to cling to our darkness and shut out the rest of the world, or we can choose to open wide the doors for Christ.

The impact a father has on the life of his child is so important. The embrace of a father can provide security and strength. Not all of us have a loving, active, earthly father. My heart grieves for those of you who were hurt by a father figure. God wants to remind you of His unconditional love for you. He will never leave you or forsake you. God stands in the gap when earthly fathers fail. God sees you. He cares. And He extends a hand for you to grasp at all times!

FIND THE ROOT

Spend a moment and let God father you. Listen carefully to your heart. In the Gospel of John, Jesus assures us that we can hear Him, "My sheep hear my voice." Remember, words of condemnation do not come from the Father.

If God brings you to it, He will bring you through it. Have you stumbled upon something in your life that you are desperate for God to see you through? Are you in the middle of something so difficult you wonder if God can get you to the other side? Has your world been turned upside down? God promises He will never leave you or forsake you. Draw close to Him and He will draw close to you. He *will* see you through any trial, burden, or life-shattering situation. His mercies are new every morning.

Chapter Fifteen

A GOOD SURPRISE

My mind was consumed with concerns about telling my children of our new family. They were ten, eight, six, and five years old at the time. I felt like I did the night we lost my Bub, "I'm not old enough to handle this!"

INTERPRETING DREAMS

It was one thing to welcome these people into my own life, but the life of my children? That was a different ballgame. So I did all I knew to do. I prayed, "Seriously, God? I have to tell them this? And just how do You suppose I go about it?"

I felt a sense of urgency but also desired God's perfect timing. I will never forget the Sunday after meeting John and Nancy at the Deli. During worship, I felt strongly that the Lord suggested, "Tell your oldest, Eli, first, and tell him alone." I wasn't sure about His reason for this, but I was certain God knew what He was talking about.

That night, I had one of the most vivid dreams of my life. I dreamt that Eli and I sat across from each other in the sitting area of my bedroom. I told him, "You know, sometimes we get surprises in life. We might get a phone call that is either a good surprise or a bad surprise. Well, Mommy got a phone call that was a *good* surprise!"

My dream then flashed to another scene. Eli slouched in his chair, let out a loud sigh, and said, "Hmmm, cool."

I woke up, sat up in bed, and asked, "God, did you just give me the beginning and the end of my conversation with Eli?"

I felt as though He answered, "Yes, and I will give you the middle as you go."

The dream was so real. It was as though God was reassuring me of Eli's wellbeing by the end of the conversation. However, I wasn't prepared for the middle part of the conversation and how much I would be required to rely on God.

The next day I went to John's house to borrow pictures of all my new family members. I thought pictures might help the kids put faces with the names of their new grandparents, aunts, and uncles. In a matter of days, equipped with a few ideas and a very vivid dream, I was ready. At least, I thought I was ready. The only problem was that Scott was out of town for the rest of the week. I called him to explain how I may not be able to sleep until I talked to the kids. He agreed I should go ahead and initiate the conversation without him.

When evening came, I told the kids I needed to have a talk with Eli alone. I directed the other three to play and to not interrupt us for any reason. Eli and I walked back to my bedroom. I sat Eli down in the chair across from me, just like I did in the dream. I strategically placed the photos face down on the table in between us.

I started, "Eli, you know how we can get surprises in life? Some surprises are good and some are not good. When we got the phone call that Uncle Bub died, that was a bad surprise. Well, Mommy recently got a good surprise."

As vaguely as possible, I enlightened him about biological parents and what that means. I reminded him that his Nanny and PaPa split up before I was born. I explained that during their separation, Nanny was dating someone named John. I tried to appear positive as I said, "All this time, we thought PaPa was my biological father, but I just found out that John is my biological father."

I could tell it wasn't going well by his physical reaction. He sat back in his chair, his lip quivered, and his eyes filled with tears. With tight lips he said, "This does not sound like a good surprise!"

My answer came without thought. "Oh, but the reason it is not bad is because no one has died. We haven't lost anyone and no one is hurt. We just gained more family, not less!"

The conversation continued to spiral as I labored to convince him that everything was fine while trying to convince myself of the same thing. I told Eli about our new family members. I shared about his Uncle Luke. I asked if he wanted to see their pictures.

"No."

He was not going to accept this easily.

He asked some extremely difficult questions, and I did my best to answer them in a way a ten-year-old brain could understand. I knew he was not ready for the answers to the technical questions he asked. I needed a diversion, and fast. I flipped one of the pictures over. It worked. It grabbed his attention.

"Is that them?"

He picked up the stack of photos and asked me to tell him all about this new family. Something shifted in his little spirit. They suddenly became *people* to him, no longer some mythical creatures coming to ruin his life.

I helped him process this information as more questions surfaced. Suddenly, he flopped back in his chair, tossed the pictures on the side table, and threw his hands up in the air. He summed up our conversation in one statement. Exhausted, he sighed, "So basically what you are telling me is that we are all screwed up!"

I laughed at his bluntness, "Yes! We are. It's exactly why we need God to help fix our messes and be our Savior!"

I can't say this was the exact reenactment of my dream. It was quite comical. There was such truth that spilled forth from his young mouth. Why yes, thank you, we are all screwed up. Thankfully, Eli came around by the end of our conversation. He realized everything was going to be fine.

I told Eli that I felt God wanted me to tell him first so he could give me ideas about how to tell the other three kids. He said, "I know! Let's sit them down on the couch and say, 'Surprise! We have a whole new family!'" I agreed that sounded like a great idea, but also that I needed to give them a little background before he made such a declaration.

Eli and I went into the living room and called for all the kids to gather. By this time, their curiosity was at an all-time high. Because they were too young to grasp the biological details of our scenario, I kept it as simple as possible, focusing on the surprise element. I also tried to correlate our situation with families who have adopted children. Their questions ranged in complexity:

"Is Nanny your Mom?"

"So PaPa is not your Dad?"

"Nanny was married before?"

"So you were adopted?"

"How do you not know who your dad is?"

I had my work cut out for me. I didn't wait long before showing them pictures of their new family. I figured the quicker we could get past the explanations, the better off we would all be, especially me. I needed a breather. Plus, the sooner I guided them past their initial shock, the sooner they could start accepting our new normal. I shared the names of their new family as I showed them the pictures.

One question arose that took the attention off any other tough questions. My kids fretted over what to call their new grandparents. They decided to take a vote. Ean ran into the kitchen and grabbed a piece of paper and a pencil. The kids yelled out potential names as he jotted them down. Nancy was already called "Nana" by her grandson, Wendy's son. We didn't have a "Nana" in our family, so we agreed they should just stick with calling her that, too. But John was called "PaPa" by Wendy's son. My kids already had a "PaPa." My dad. We agreed it would be too confusing to call both their grandfathers by the same name. Also, we concluded that they only had one "PaPa," and that's how it should stay. It was nonnegotiable. We had to call John something different.

Ean began writing down a few grandpa names. I would be lying if I told you I didn't steer them in the direction I wanted. I really desired a name that I might eventually call John myself. I thought it would be too confusing for my children if I ever called John "Dad." But I could see myself eventually calling him something more personal than his first name. We narrowed it down and took a vote. We all agreed. John was officially my family's one and only "Pops!"

After the name decision, my seven-year-old daughter sat back on the couch and started to sob. I knew something was going on in her little mind, and I needed to know what it was. I took her to my room. I didn't want what she was feeling to possibly influence my boys' current state of contentment. I sat Ella down and asked, "Sweetie, what did you think of? What made you cry all of a sudden as we were talking about Nana and Pops?"

In her innocent, sweet voice she softly wept, "I am just going to miss Nanny and PaPa!"

My heart broke for her little heart. I scooped her up in my arms and quickly reassured her, "Nanny and PaPa are not going anywhere! We will still see them all the time. They will always be in your life."

In her confused little mind, she thought we were "switching" grandparents. She thought we were replacing PaPa and Nanny with Pops and Nana. I grabbed my phone and let her call my parents. I thought hearing their voices would ease her worry.

I was beyond relieved when these initial conversations were over, but I wasn't naive enough to believe this one conversation would answer all their questions. One day, this vague explanation is not going to be sufficient, especially for my intuitive daughter. A couple of times over the past few years, a question has popped up. But thankfully, this new family is such a part of their normal life now that they really don't seem to question much. After this first conversation, I felt like I leapt a tall building in a single bound. And now I could breathe. Now we could start our new life with our new bonus grandparents.

MEETING POPS AND NANA

I knew John and Nancy were eager to meet their four new grandkids. In just three weeks, one letter, and a DNA test, they went from having one grandkid to five! My kids needed time to let the news settle. The more I mentioned Pops and Nana, the more my kids asked to meet them. We eventually called to invite them to our house. I thought it would be best if Pops and Nana came over to our house to meet the kids. My kids would feel more comfortable in their own home. I hoped it would make the unusual situation less uncomfortable.

Most of my kids were excited. However, Eli was not too sure about gaining more grandparents. He was pretty content with his PaPa and Nanny. This was not surprising, since he is my child who doesn't handle change very well. But whether he liked it or not, Pops and Nana were coming.

On the day of the visit, the kids peered out the window, watching for a car to pull into our driveway. Pops and Nana did not keep them waiting long. As soon as they saw them pull up, Ean, Ella, and Ezra ran out the door and into the yard. Eli was going to make it a little tougher, and I had to call for him to come.

I considered correcting the three runners to slow down, hoping they wouldn't overwhelm John and Nancy. Instead, I decided to let them be. Why pretend they are something they are not—the Von Trapps. I was shocked to see Ezra make a dash for Pops. I think John was even more surprised. While John was still in the street, Ezra bounced into his arms! A huge smile spread across John's face and he kissed Ezra. It was more wonderful than I could have planned. The Holy Spirit was at work.

Even so, I almost corrected Ezra again. But this time it was out of a sense of protection. I wasn't trying to protect John. He perfectly handled a five-year-old jumping into his arms. I felt a sense of protection for my daddy. Selfishly, I wanted to say, "Don't be that excited to see John, save that for your PaPa."

I thought to myself, "I am so glad my parents didn't see this!"

I worried about how it would make them feel. It sounds silly, but it felt like I was letting my kids cheat on my parents. My heart was in conflict. A part of me was excited for the kids to meet Pops and Nana. I wanted them to feel comfortable, just not too comfortable.

Because of grace, in a matter of moments, all those thoughts exited my mind and I was able to relax and enjoy the moment. John and Nancy needed to see my kids excited about meeting them. Can you even imagine what they were feeling? Can you imagine the intimidation they must have felt? I am thankful my kids gave them a grand welcome.

We welcomed them into our home and, essentially, into our hearts. They sat on the couch as they tried to absorb what was happening around them. John and Nancy interacted with the kids beautifully. Every once in a while, a different child would sit somewhere near them on the couch. I could tell John and Nancy enjoyed that sign of affection. Even Eli made an appearance a time or two. John and Nancy seemed thrilled as they tried to learn a little about each one of the kids.

After a few hours, John and Nancy grew fidgety and decided to head home. I thought it was because they did not want to overstay their welcome. After all, they had just met me. They had no idea that I am actually a come-early-stay-late kind of person. Later, as I got to know them, I realized

John and Nancy do not get out much, and when they do get out, they don't stay long.

As John and Nancy stood up to leave, my kids gave them big hugs. We are a very affectionate family. We all kindly and gently accepted one another with each embrace. Pops and Nana would turn out to be big huggers themselves. We walked Pops and Nana to their car. I stood in the yard and gave Nancy a huge hug. I quietly asked her, "How are you doing with all of this?"

She sweetly answered, "Well, I am a little overwhelmed with how large our family got overnight, but I absolutely love you! I am so thankful you are in our family."

I was humbled by her response. Of all people, she should have been the one with major issues. Even if she had dealt with Rejection in her life, it didn't make her reject in return. She chose to accept me, and thus received the good fruit acceptance bears. Because she was a believer in Jesus Christ, she saw things like He would. She was gracious and forgiving, welcoming and warm.

WHAT MATTERS

There are situations and conversations we need help navigating. We might call a mentor or a friend to ask for advice. We might head to the bookstore to find an encouraging book. We should not be shy to ask for help. My situation seemed impossible to manage, so I asked the One I knew had an answer for everything.

Sometimes we need to attack our situation head on. Sometimes we need to take our time and let things happen naturally. In my case, I needed to exercise both approaches. No matter the path we take, we could all use a little wisdom, am I right?

FIND THE ROOT

Do you need a word of wisdom from the Lord? Are you facing a situation that seems overwhelming? Ask God, and He will give creative ideas, sometimes even step-by-step instructions. God is big enough to provide for your life at every moment!

Have you had to face a "new normal" lately? No matter how sudden or gradual the change occurs, it can often be hard to handle. The fact that John's wife was gracious, forgiving, and accepting helped to usher peace into this complex situation. How can you choose acceptance and graciousness in your life?

Chapter Sixteen

NEW YORK, NEW YORK

So what's life supposed to look like now? I was asking that question just as much as everyone else. In a matter of months, I had a new family. I was spending as much time as possible with John (Pops), Nancy (Nana), and Wendy. Not only did I want to get to know them, I figured they would want to get to know me, too. I brought over albums of photos from my wedding, my children's baby books, and anything else I thought they would find interesting. They too would pull albums off shelves and introduce me to all my family members. We shared stories from the past. We tried to fill in the gaps for one another.

FUMBLING TOWARD FAMILIARITY

During the first few months of our new familial relationship, I felt very heavy-hearted for John. He seemed to be having a difficult time with everything. During our visits, he would often cry and grow silent. I could only assume he was dealing with his own shock, regret, and shame. I wanted time alone with him, but it seemed almost impossible. John and Nancy really didn't do anything without one another. I was enjoying getting to know Nancy, but I really wanted to talk to just my father for a while. One day, Wendy offered to take her mom to breakfast so I could go to breakfast with just John.

I met him for breakfast with the goal of getting to know him better. This turned out to be the only time I would be alone with him. I was able to talk with him about things I thought might make Nancy uncomfortable. I wasn't trying to be secretive, but respectful, of Nancy. I wanted to ask him about his memories from 1972. I wanted to ask him about his relationship with my mom. I didn't think Nancy would want to be any part of that conversation. John reluctantly answered me as simply as possible. He wasn't used to being asked such direct questions. I learned quickly that trying to get him to open up was like pulling teeth. He definitely didn't offer any unprompted answers. That morning, I realized I was going to have to be content with a much simpler relationship with him than I hoped for. He had a sweet, tender heart, but I also sensed a pretty impenetrable shell on the outside. I tried to encourage him like I would anyone I saw struggling. I reminded him that forgiving himself would make a world of difference. I'm not so sure he agreed, or even totally understood.

He thought keeping his feelings and emotions to himself was being strong.

I thought it kept him bound to his regret.

In the beginning, the phone calls were frequent. We talked several times each week. Every conversation would end with Pops saying, "Okay, now you be careful!" Eventually an "I love you, baby." would be added to his phrase. Since I spent so much time getting to know my new family, I felt the only missing piece of the puzzle was meeting my little brother, Luke.

IRREPLACEABLE

I always had a secret bucket list wish. I desperately wanted to celebrate my fortieth birthday in New York City. Since my birthday is on New Year's Eve, it always seemed like it would be the celebration of celebrations. It just so happened that my big birthday was coming up, and my new brother owned an apartment in Queens. Wendy and Luke discussed the idea of us sisters coming to see him. Wendy and I decided to go to New York to commemorate our 40th birthdays that were only a few months apart. After making a few arrangements, Wendy and I were off to New York to meet my little brother.

As Wendy and I sat on the plane, we chatted about what was to come. We talked mostly about Luke. I asked so many questions. Even through her excitement, my spirit could sense an underlying sadness in her. For a moment, I put myself in her shoes. I thought about how much I adored my Bub, Eric. I wondered how I would have felt if some other girl came out of the woodwork and said, "Hey, I'm Eric's sister, too, and you are going to have to share!" I was already used to sharing my Bub with my sister. But for Wendy, this was her only brother, her only sibling. I knew I needed to speak to her heart.

When we were close to landing, I shifted in my seat to face Wendy. I looked at her with compassion in my eyes and said, "Wendy, there is something I need you to hear me say. No matter what happens between Luke and me, I will never come between you and him. I will never try to outdo you. I will never try to have a better relationship with him than you. I would have had a hard time sharing my Bub, and I feel for you. If we let him, the enemy will try to twist things and attack us in this area. Don't let him."

She exhaled loudly and with relief. Tears welled up in her eyes and she quickly responded, "Thank you for saying that. I truly believe you are one of the best things that has ever happened to this family. However, the thought of sharing Luke has been the hardest part for me."

We made a pact to be vigilant in thinking the best of one another during our trip.

When the plane finally hit the runway, I thought I might hyperventilate! I handed my camera to Wendy and asked her to take pictures. I said, "I know you are going to want to run and hug him, but just this once, will you stay back and capture our meeting with pictures?"

She totally agreed that this was a moment that could not be re-made: a sister would be meeting her brother for the very first time at almost forty years old!

I'm sure we weren't in the farthest terminal, but it sure seemed like it as I wheeled my suitcase anxiously down the path. I turned the corner and saw people waiting and greeting their beloved travelers. Then, I spotted him. He was wearing a black button-down shirt and jeans. We locked eyes, and I made a beeline for him. I don't know who lifted their hands first, but in an instant I was hugging my little brother. *My little brother!* The hug didn't feel particularly warm; however, we *were* technically strangers.

What really took my breath away was our uncanny resemblance. He looked like me. The photos I'd seen of him didn't do our resemblance justice. In every recent picture I saw of him, he was always wearing glasses or a hat. Growing up, I was always told, "You and Shawna don't look alike, but she and Eric do." When I found out about Wendy, I daydreamed about the possibility of having a sister who looks like me. And what if she has mannerisms like me? What if she talks with her hands like me? But these dreams were never realized because, just like Shawna, Wendy and I didn't share the same blood. With Luke, I never considered the possibility of our physical resemblance. But here I was in front of him, and something about him made me feel I was looking in a mirror.

I think it was his eyes. Something about his eyes reminded me of my own. I wanted to stare at him, but he seemed unsure and uncertain around me. I turned and saw his wife, Jennifer. Like Wendy, she stepped back to allow us our moment. She approached me, and we met with a hug. More hugs were exchanged with Wendy, and the four of us huddled around with big smiles on our faces. They asked about our flight as they helped us gather our luggage. Once we had our things, we headed to their car.

As we loaded our bags, I admitted to Luke, "There are a ton of people back home just waiting for a picture of us together. Can we take one?"

He agreed.

I enthusiastically asked, "Do you not think we look alike?"

He looked at me, and with a laugh said, "Yeah, kind of."

We smiled, and *click*, the picture was taken. Wendy and I climbed in the back seat, and we were off. I made a few big-eyed faces to Wendy as I looked down at the photo. She too was amazed by the resemblance. I stared at the picture and sent out a few texts. My happy photo was received by friends and family with lots of tears. They too were shocked by our resemblance.

THE GREATEST CITY IN THE WORLD

On our first day, we hit the city running. And by running I mean Wendy and I tried to keep up with Luke and Jennifer. I wasn't sure if they were just classic New Yorkers and rushing like everyone else, or if they were trying to make sure we covered as much ground as possible. Regardless, around the fourth hour of touring Staten Island, my hunger overtook me. It was late afternoon, and Wendy and I hadn't eaten since our early morning breakfast. I grabbed Wendy and whispered, "Do these people eat? I need food. Now. I feel sick."

So we stopped to eat at a little deli. We all ordered food and sat down at a round table. I found it odd that my new brother and I had spent hours together without any meaningful conversation. I know that if someone told me they were my long lost sibling, I would not spend the first four hours nearly running the streets of New York. I would grab a famous street hot dog, find the nearest park bench, and start the conversation (then again, I'm a girl).

I threw some bait, "So do you want to know anything? Do you want to know, like, how I am your sister?"

It wasn't Luke who fired the first question. Jennifer wasted no time, "Why now? Why are you just coming forward with this information?"

Her question stunned me. It was evident they were completely uninformed about the entire situation. They thought I knew about John's paternity my entire life and just suddenly decided to break the news forty years later. Over the next few minutes, I explained how I came to this discovery merely a few months ago. I let them know that this was a shock to me and my family as well as to the Prestons.

I was perplexed. Why wasn't anything really explained to Luke? Because Luke thought this had been kept secret for forty years, he thought his dad knew about his paternity. Knowing John's character, Luke could not figure out why he would have abandoned me. John would never abandon his child. I was grateful to clear the confusion. I explained that John knew my mom was pregnant, but she was convinced I was Freddie's baby. The conversation ended almost as quickly as it started. Luke and Jennifer seemed content with the amount of information I shared and didn't ask any other questions. This conversation, to my surprise, ended up being the only "serious" conversation that would take place the entire trip.

With this being my first time in New York, I was torn between wanting to focus on my brother and wanting to check a few things off my bucket list. This trip was a dream come true, but I wanted to get to know my little brother more. I assumed we would be asking lots of questions, trying to get to know one another. I thought we might talk about our childhoods and memories. I thought he might want to know about my family. I thought he might ask about his nephews and niece. But after our first day in the city, I realized these conversations may happen later. He seemed like a kind man, very attentive to his wife. I didn't have ill feelings toward him. Wanting to give him the benefit of the doubt, I concluded that communication isn't his strong suit. Knowing Luke may happen slowly. But I was in New York, and I was determined Wendy and I were going to have a good time!

We spent the next week touring New York and hanging out at Luke's apartment. If any part of this story leaves me hoping for more, it's this relationship. Although we look alike, our personalities couldn't be more different. I found my brother to be introverted, reserved, yet caring. To be honest,

I do not think he knew what to do with me. I can come off really strong. I am a total extrovert. I tried to get to know him by asking him questions. But the questions I could ask were limited. The details of his job were off limits due to its private nature. Luke didn't have children at the time, which could have created a bond. The main thing I asked about were his travels. Luke and Jennifer went on some really amazing trips. This topic seemed to stir enthusiasm in Luke. I loved hearing his excitement as he shared about their adventures. I even looked through many of his photos.

I decided to show him pictures of my own. I told him all about his three nephews and niece. I thought he might want to become familiar with them, knowing they would all meet one day.

While we hung out, I observed Luke and Wendy's relationship. The bar was set high for them, as I compared other sibling relationships to the relationship I had with my brother (although that probably wasn't fair). I wondered about their friendship. I later learned that Wendy moved out when Luke was only ten years old. Their distance in both age and location caused a natural disconnect between them. I noticed Wendy was the one to ignite many new discussions. When I told her I wasn't convinced Luke liked me, she assured me it wasn't personal. She confirmed what I suspected: Luke was more reserved, quiet. She too still worked on strengthening their bond. It made me realize what I had with my brother isn't typical, but was a once in a lifetime relationship.

My bucket list dream came true. I experienced New York City, in Times Square, for my fortieth birthday. Not everything happened the way I envisioned, but in the end, meeting the last member of my new family was satisfying. I did leave feeling a little insecure about my relationship with Luke. But with

God, I know all things are possible so I remained hopeful that a deeper relationship would develop in the future.

WHAT MATTERS

Even in the best circumstances, there is always something that may not turn out like you had hoped. It is how we respond, or how we allow it to influence us, that will make all the difference in our lives.

Some of you, too, have experienced a reunion that did not turn out quite like you envisioned. Sometimes relationships click instantaneously, others take time to grow. For those situations, I want to deposit into your heart what God deposited into mine. He says to all of us, "I am a big God in every circumstance, at every moment. Even when I seem far or absent, I am the same! I am good all the time and in every circumstance!"

Begin to look beyond your circumstances. God's ways are always higher than ours. He is always working things out for good.

FIND THE ROOT

Sometimes our attitudes are the only variable that can shift in a situation. We can't change others, but we can change ourselves. Ask God for a fresh perspective. Changing how we act or respond can make all the difference in the world.

Being expectant is totally different than having expectations. Unmet expectations often lead to disappointment or frustration. Being expectant is a more hopeful mindset. Is there an area in your life where you need to lay down expectations and pick up an expectant heart?

Chapter Seventeen

OPEN HEART SURGERY

In May 2014, almost two years after meeting my new family, I traveled to Guatemala with a group of women. It was a trip specifically designed for the female leaders in our church. The group was called Women in Leadership Development (W.I.L.D.). Little did I know, that trip would be instrumental in God's call to write the book you are now reading.

I sat in a session in which the teacher talked about "leading whole and holy." She encouraged us to awaken our souls to make sure we weren't in denial about anything. She reminded us that we all have a story, but that some of us haven't been honest with ourselves about a portion of our own story. Honestly, I was only half-listening, as I thought this particular subject didn't pertain to me. In hindsight, I should have known my attitude placed a target right smack dab in the middle of my heart. One of my greatest stories was unfolding before my eyes over the last few years. And *I was just fine with everything.*

I should have known better. Often, the second we think, "I got this, God," He will download something in our spirit about the very subject we think doesn't pertain to us. At the end of her lesson, the speaker asked us to bow our heads and get alone with God. She said, "Ask God if you are in denial about any part of your story."

THIS ISN'T WHAT I ASKED FOR

As I prayed, God used His divine scalpel to perform spiritual open heart surgery. As the prompting question crossed my mind, something settled in my spirit, rocking me to my core. I felt God say, "Sweet daughter, you haven't admitted that you didn't *want* a new family. You were happy with your other family. You *want* your Bub back, and you weren't expecting a new brother. You wish things could go back to the way they were."

My face grew hot with emotion. My heart began to pound. I dropped my head down, and the tears poured. I mourned. God was right. He peeled back a hidden layer of my heart. These last few years were filled with such an exhilarating journey of The Days of Dana's Life. I was so busy accepting and rejoicing over the new normal, I never completely grieved the loss of my old normal. Over the years since my brother's death, I wrestled to find contentment in life without my Bub. But in order to live "whole and holy," I needed to face all my emotions. Even though this story was a happy one, I now had an entire new family I never asked for. Like it or not, my life would never be the same.

The next day, we were told to find a place to be alone with God. They encouraged us to let Him speak to us about our story. I gathered my belongings and wandered outside. We were staying at the most amazing resort I've ever seen. I walked along the sidewalk, admiring the view. Either way I looked, I saw volcanoes dotting the horizon. Our resort was next to a golf course, and we were surrounded by perfectly manicured grass. No matter where I looked, my eyes beheld the majesty of God's creation. I spotted a lone bench on the edge of the golf course, and it was calling my name. It felt like God saved this seat for me. Past the rolling hills of the golf course was an active volcano. To my surprise (and slight fear), it would let off a little smoke here and there. For me, there was no better place to be alone with God. I was right in the middle of His creation, and I could *feel* Him.

As I prayed, unexpected anger pierced through me. I questioned God, "Why me? Why did you choose me for this story? Why did you give me a new family?"

He whispered, "I knew I could trust you with this unique story. As you share this story, I know you will always point back to Me. I know you will give Me all the glory."

My anger immediately subsided and a peace overwhelmed me. I wanted to honor God by sharing my story and giving Him all the glory.

STEPPING OUT IN FAITH

At the end of the week, I finally verbalized what God asked me to do: write my story. This was a big deal for me. Nearly every time I told someone my story for the first time, they would say, "This needs to be a book!"

In my heart I knew they were right, but my head would never fail to convince me otherwise. After all, I am *not* a writer. I don't even *like* writing. "Author" was never a title I desired or even thought possible to obtain. But there, hundreds of miles away in Guatemala, I stood in front of a room full of the most loving ladies and declared, "I am supposed to write a book!"

The very next day, I sat on the porch of my hotel room. It was raining, the kind of rain that pours fast and hard, then stops abruptly. I opened my journal and grabbed a pen. I asked God to help me write an outline of the book He had in mind. As quickly as the rains poured, the words poured through my pen and onto the page. I wrote for the next two hours, rarely retiring my pen for a break. The detailed outline flowed forth from my mind as if someone else was thinking it. It felt supernatural.

I returned home from that trip a new woman. God completed a work in my heart I didn't know I needed. I also knew He was going to help me during the next part of my journey: gathering my story into book form.

As I write my last chapter, I am reminded of God's faithfulness. He was faithful to me as He knit me together in the womb of my young mom who was in a less than ideal situation. He was faithful to me as I grew up questioning my truth. He was faithful to me as I was painfully rejected several times early in life. He was faithful to me as I searched for freedom in areas of darkness and sin. He was faithful to me as my heart healed from all the tragedies I experienced. He was faithful to me every step of the way as truth unfolded.

Just as faithful as He was and is to me, He is faithful to you, too.

WHEN BLOOD MATTERS

For over a year, I prayed to receive the title of this book God planted in my heart. One night, I woke up from a dead sleep. I don't know if I spoke the words out loud or just replayed them in my head, but I heard the phrase "when blood matters." I opened my eyes and tried to wake up in order to keep up with my thoughts.

Blood does matter at times, but sometimes it doesn't. If you need a blood transfusion, it is extremely important to know your exact blood type or problems can arise. In the case of adoption, it doesn't matter that the parents and child do not share the same blood. The fact that I do not share the same blood as my sister or daddy does not matter. But my blood type *did* matter in discovering the truth about my biological father.

Throughout this whole journey one truth resounded: the blood that matters most is the blood we share in Jesus Christ. When we accept Him as our Savior here on earth, we accept the sacrifice He made as He shed His blood for our sins. We receive a blood transfusion from the Son of God. His blood secures our place in heaven for all eternity!

To God be all the glory for the great things He has done!

WHAT MATTERS

So there it is. My story. It is the good, the bad, and the ugly. It is my heart and soul poured out over these pages. Truth is, we all have a story. God will use our tests in life to become our testimony. When we share our testimony, we give God the glory He so perfectly deserves. What the enemy hopes will destroy us, God is eager to use for our good.

Everything I went through had great potential to send me down a destructive path, a path that would have resulted in a totally different life than the one I am currently living. Instead, I allowed God to perform His mighty redemptive work!

FIND THE ROOT

Do you have a story the Lord has been calling you to share, or maybe even to write? Consider how God may be asking you to share your unique story for His glory.

Are you in denial about a part of your story or testimony? Is there something you are ignoring in hopes that it will go away? Get quiet and ask God if there is anything He wants to speak with you about. Ask him to heal any fears, wounds, or worries that He may bring to your attention.

Lana and Freddie
while they were dating.

John and Lana dating.
This is the picture I saw in my 20s
that caused me to question even more.

Dana (3 ½) , Eric (5 ½)
and Shawna (4 mos).

Late 1980s when
Bub's appearance began
to change even more.

Best day of my life!

The day I met
John and Nancy.

The day my kids met their Pops
and Nana for the first time.

The day in New York I met
my new brother, Luke.

Christmas 2015. John and Nancy joined our family Christmas party.

My Family

Epilogue

WHERE ARE WE NOW?

I know what most of you are thinking. What does it all look like now? What is life like five years later? Let me fill you in, my friend. Nothing much has changed. I like to think my life and heart have just expanded.

MY MOM AND DAD

Of course, nothing changed with my parents. My relationship with them is still the same as it always was. This situation never altered my opinions of them. I still celebrate the same holidays and family events with them. My parents did decide to go out of town for Thanksgiving the first year I met the Prestons. I wasn't sure if it was intentional, but it freed me to spend our first Thanksgiving getting to know my new family. I was free from having to choose one over the other.

At first, I don't think any of the parents were eager to spend time together. Not because of ill feelings, but because of the fragile circumstances. As it turns out, it was all water under the bridge. After everything settled down, the grandparents' hearts began to soften.

Consider the situation. Just as Wendy and I lived parallel stories, so did our parents! Both my mother and Nana gave birth to daughters who they thought were one man's child but turned out to be wrong. Both my father and Pops raised daughters they thought were their biological girls. They both found out, via the same DNA test, that their daughters had the DNA of another man! So really, no one was in a place to be judgmental. They were all in the same boat, paddling with the same oars. They could truly empathize with one another, leading them to extend grace.

They began to see each other in a new light, and not as "the other woman" or "the other man." Since they shared grandkids, there wasn't time for nonsense. My parents and John and Nancy often sat next to each other at my kids' events! I invited John and Nancy to my house on Christmas Eve to celebrate with about thirty of my family members. For the last two years, they've taken me up on my offer and we've all loved it! My family and extended family welcome them into our crazy house. That's how we roll. It's not awkward unless you make it awkward! That's what my mama taught me.

My daddy has been nothing but precious throughout this whole process. He read this book with such humility. He even went so far as to apologize for not being more present during my younger years. It allowed him to enter another level of freedom, releasing him of any guilt and shame. I thanked him for more than compensating during my later years.

While this story has been hard for my mom to read (understandably so), she has been nothing but supportive. It was hard for me to let my parents read it. I wanted to keep our focus on the good God created out of our mess. We continually remind ourselves that while the past was full of confusion and pain, we are all healing in our present!

JOHN AND NANCY

I like to refer to them as "bonus" parents and grandparents. That first year, I spent a lot of time trying to get to know them. John called me a lot and let me know if I hadn't called him enough, too. Pops, as I call him, feels like a father figure, but not like my *dad*. It's not that anything is wrong in the relationship. It's just that I've had the same dad for forty years. That's a role not easily shared with someone I recently met. Pops seems to understand that. But, just as I suspected, he instantly felt like a relative. He is sweet and will ask, "How's your mom and dad doing?" He always honors their role in my life. He never fails to finish our conversations with an "I love you" and "Now you be careful, baby." I love it. It makes me feel like he is taking care of me.

Pops and Nana have been very intentional with birthdays. In five years, they have never forgotten a grandkids' birthday. That's impressive! They will drop by or mail a card with money for them. My kids have grown to count on their visits and cards from Pops and Nana! On one of my recent birthdays, I noticed something sitting outside on my porch. I opened the door to find flowers and a card. I opened the card and read these words:

"There once was a beautiful girl who grew up to be so sweet and thoughtful and caring, that wherever she went people would say, 'She must be an angel in disguise!' Not only do I know that angel personally, but I am lucky enough to have her as my daughter."

It was signed, "Pops." My heart leapt and tears streamed down my face. That meant more to me than he will ever know.

As the years have passed, the number of visits and phone calls has decreased. My busy life seemed to frustrate Pops. He found it difficult to understand a life filled with running a house and coordinating the schedules of six people. He struggled to find a good time to reach me. On my part, I tried not to allow much time to pass before contacting him.

For the past five years, I have honored him on Father's Day. I stop by for a visit, give a gift, or at least call him. But this most recent Father's Day was different. I felt an unrelenting nudge to take him to breakfast. I called to set up a date. I thought I might be eating with both Pops and Nana, since I hadn't been alone with him since our very first father-daughter breakfast. I pulled into the driveway and there stood Pops, alone and wearing a nice shirt. For the first half of breakfast we caught up with one another. But about halfway through our meal, our conversation took a more serious turn. Pops was open and vulnerable, just what I longed for during the first few years. He admitted he struggled being around me. He confessed through tears that he felt he abandoned my mom while pregnant with his child. He assumed this is what everyone else thought when they saw him. I was flabbergasted! I fumbled as I tried to explain that no one thought that but him! I re-emphasized the fact that you can't abandon a child you didn't know was yours. This proved my suspicions that he was living in guilt and shame, and therefore unable to truly bond with me.

So for the last half of breakfast, through numerous tears, I encouraged him with every fiber of my being. This book was almost complete, but I felt this detail pertinent to add. It has brought clarity to so many things. It serves as yet another example of someone believing a lie, letting it rule their life, and ultimately hindering any chance of a deeper relationship with a loved one.

I believe everything happens for a reason. My prayer is that my Pops will be able to receive forgiveness, forgive himself, and live the rest of his life in peace. If God calls us to the one, Pops is my one! That vulnerable conversation was a kiss from heaven as I was able to peer deep into my father's heart for the first time.

WENDY

My "bonus" sister has been the sweetest part of my story. She is always a breath of fresh air. When I call to vent about life, she always listens and assures me she understands. The saddest part is that I don't get to be with her very much. She has a high-pressure job that keeps her busy, not to mention she is a wife and a mom, too. Our time together is precious but unfortunately rare. My kids call her "Aunt Wendy," and I couldn't be happier about it.

Initially, when Wendy told John about the results of the DNA test, they shared a sweet moment similar to the one I shared with my dad. John did shed a few tears, but through his tears he said, "You have been my girl since the day you were born. You are mine!" He reiterated that nothing was going to change between them.

Remember Wendy's biological father, the one who died in a car accident before she was even one year old? Well, Wendy decided to dig a little deeper into her truth. She was shocked as she read Tom's obituary. At the very bottom it stated he left behind a two-year-old daughter! That meant Wendy had a sister who was two years older! Wendy, of course, wanted to reach out to her. She sent Ruth a letter sealed with prayers.

Wendy was thrilled when her sister responded. Ruth's mother never had any more children after losing Tom. Ruth told Wendy, "I have always wanted a sibling, but my mother never had any more children! I have never been a sister, but I will do my best to be a sister to you."

So Wendy didn't gain one sister during this adventure, she gained two!

LUKE

In the very beginning, it seemed like my new brother and I were going to build a relationship. I sensed he was making an effort to know us. He actually came to town that first Thanksgiving to meet his nephews and niece, which was very kind. Admittedly, I made more effort in the beginning, too. I sent him a birthday gift. He gave my kids Christmas money.

But in the second year, he and Jennifer welcomed their first baby, and we all know how time consuming a new baby can be! He visited a couple of times over the course of the following two years. I was sad that I only got to see him and meet my niece for about an hour the entire time they were in town.

As I wrote this book, the Lord convicted me. My heart has become a little hardened to this particular situation. God began to open my eyes and heart to new possibilities in the future. This past year, Luke, Jennifer, and their daughter all came to visit for a week. I was thrilled and blessed to be part of their time here. The whole family came over to my house for an afternoon visit. My kids hung out with their cousin! I got to spend time with my niece. I now have a much better attitude about the whole situation. It is hard to have a long distance relationship with someone you just met, even if you are siblings. I am now content with any time I get to spend with Luke and his family. Luke and I don't have a past, but I am believing we *do* have a future!

ACKNOWLEDGMENTS

To Daddy—Our relationship is so sweet. I admire so much about you. You are kind and steady. You live to serve your family. I am thankful you raised me. Sharing Jesus' blood makes our bond all the more important, the only blood that really matters!

To Mom—You changed our family's destiny. By accepting Jesus, you literally led our family in a completely opposite direction. My life is a direct result of your decision. Thank you for saying yes to Jesus! You never made me feel anything but loved, accepted, and adored.

To Bub—I miss your voice. I miss your dimples. Thankfully, I will see you again one day!

To Sis—Of course I love you, but I also *like* you. Thank you for being my steady anchor. Your tender reaction changed my heart in an instant! It was healing.

To Pops—Thank you for wrapping me in your arms and eventually into your heart. Your acceptance was exactly what my heart needed.

To Nana—You are a treasure! Your character is undeniably straight from God. Thank you for loving and accepting me from day one. I love your warm hugs.

To Wendy—My only regret is missing thirty-nine years of getting to be your sister. You are a breath of fresh air. Thank you for loving me and making me feel so welcome in the family.

To Luke—Thanks for welcoming me into your home and being such an awesome tour guide in New York. I love the memories we have and look forward to building more.

To Nantie—Thank you for not only being my aunt, but one of my best friends! I told you nothing would change.

To Mama Sellars—Thank you for loving me as your own daughter from the moment you met me. Your prayers and encouragement have been crucial.

To my "Other Mothers" (Vickie, Debbie, and Nancy)—Some people wish for one mentor in their life, but I was privileged to have three (God knew I needed three). You have each played an irreplaceable role in my life at just the right time. I am blessed to call you my friends.

To Chrystal—See! I told you I could have been an author. Thank you for loving juicy details and making me express them to you verbally and in note form. I am certain it helped prepare me to write this book. We've been best friends for thirty-four years and you are truly a sister to me.

To the Village—Marci, we have been stuck like glue for fifteen years. We have walked many roads together. Thank you for being one of my biggest cheerleaders. **Maria**, we were like sisters the minute we met. You love so well and know how to make someone feel special. Thank you for celebrating every step I took in this process and giving up an entire week-end to help me write. **Jenn**, thank you for holding my hand through it all. You love so well. **Vickie**, you are my sunshine on a cloudy day. Thank you for every sweet encouragement. **Amanda**, you cry when I cry, but you can always make me laugh when I need to lighten up.

To Brooke—You encouraged me to write a book, and then you went and wrote one before me. God knew I needed a path to follow. Thank you for paving the perfect way for me. You never cared if I copied any of your ideas. You and Scott monetarily proved how much you believe in this project, even providing a place to get away and write for the weekend. Thank you both for loving me, believing in me, encouraging me, and helping me fund this book. You left me with no excuses. I could not have done this without you.

To The Staats—Ten years ago, when you walked in our front door, my family and I were forever blessed. You have been our teachers, mentors, marriage counselors, our children's mentors, and most importantly, our friends. Thank you for loving so deeply.

To my Gateway friends—**Laurinda**, you were the first person to ever read my original manuscript. You confirmed it should be a book. **Linda Godsey**, you valued my story so much you invited me to share my testimony in front of hundreds of people. Then, you also debuted my story in your own book, *Origins*. **Rach**, my "soulmate best friend," you were with me each step of the way, even sentence by sentence! **Marla**, you have never stopped loving and supporting me. You believe in me and our friendship. You are a deep well. **Franklin**, you offer a steady flow of love and acceptance. I never tire of seeing you dance through my yard and through my front door. **Lia**, you were involved in every step as this story unfolded. Thanks for being one of the first to read and edit my early manuscript. **Lexa**, thank you for believing in me, sister. Your encouragement changes me.

To my Guatemala girls—You all eagerly supported me as I announced I was called to write this book. Cassie, you called the scribblings on my paper a "book proposal," even when I had no clue what that meant. Jan, you were the first one to call me an author. You gave me pertinent advice, giving my book more purpose.

To Olivia Spears, my editor—You were the first person who read my book without knowing me or my story. Receiving your first round of edits validated me more than you know! Thank you for believing in this project. Your encouragement and edits were my fuel to see this through to the end. I miss you already!

To Paul Sirmon—I never realized the importance of a graphic designer until working with you on this project. You and your wife, Katrina, nailed the book cover! The upside down tree was a brilliant idea.

To all who encouraged me to write a book (there are too many to remember and too many to name)—You were the wind in my sail. We did it!

FAMILY DEBUT

Scott—You are still the one. We have been through more in our 17 years than most people go through in a lifetime. We have been shaken, but not broken. I am thankful for our covenant, as it sometimes remains the only constant. Our morning coffee dates on our front porch swing will always be my favorite!

Eli—You are the best servant. I love how you love me. You look for ways to serve me, from filling up my water cup to rubbing my shoulders if I am working. You love well. May you always stay solid in your relationship with Jesus.

Ean—You are pure joy. You give the sweetest hugs to me. You brighten up the room when you walk in. May you always remember Who blessed you with your talent and use it for His glory.

Ella—You are wise beyond your years. I love God's tender mercy in your heart. You are discerning. I'm convinced God gave me you to keep me humble. May you always keep your heart and ears tuned into the Holy Spirit.

Ezra—You are the coolest kid on the planet. You just can't help it. You are so sweet and tender to me. You will always be my baby no matter how old you get. May you always stand strong in the Lord.

DANA SELLARS is a wife and mom to four children. Her biggest task in life is managing six people's schedules and getting everyone where they need to be at the correct time. Her weeks are full of home-schooling two of her children and her weekends are always packed with activities. She has the gift of hospitality. Her home is always open to family and friends. If she doesn't have a house full of people, it is because she is at the baseball fields watching her sons play baseball. She loves to read. She loves to be involved at her church. She has a heart for missions and loves to travel. She resides in Texas.

Connect With Dana

whenbloodmatters.com

Dana Sellars

whenbloodmatters

Made in the USA
Columbia, SC
27 August 2017